LIGHT FROM ABOVE

LIGHT FROM ABOVE

A Popular Presentation of Christian Doctrine

Revised Edition

Alfred W. Koehler

CONCORDIA PUBLISHING HOUSE · SAINT LOUIS

Library of Congress Cataloging-in-Publication Data

Koehler, Alfred W.
   Light from above : a popular presentation of Christian doctrine / Alfred W. Koehler.
—Rev. ed.
      p. cm.
   ISBN 978-0-7586-3883-0
1. Theology, Doctrinal—Popular works. I. Title.
   BT77.K6 2012
   230--dc23

                                                                2012009209

1   2   3   4   5   6   7   8   9   10   21   19   18   17   16   15   14   13   12

CONTENTS

PREFACE

In writing this book the author has sought to present something that fits into the thought of life and into the heart hunger of all people.

There are, thank God, truths which are contemporary with all generations. External circumstances or the changing moods and whims of humanity do not affect the eternal verities of God's Word. The Word of God stands and is ever applicable to the problems of life and to their solution.

Within this book the Word of God is explained; and it is applied to everyday living. May it serve to bless many who are seeking after God's purpose of life!

Alfred W. Koehler
Oakland, California, June 15, 1959

CHAPTER 1

On Being Religious

All human beings are by nature religious. A study of human nature reveals this fact. They may not be affiliated with a religious organization or may not have formulated their religious convictions in a set of doctrines or a code of ethics, but all are religious nevertheless. Religion is not acquired; it is inborn. It is as natural as life itself.

The religion that man has by nature is founded on man's natural knowledge of God and of the Law of God. Man knows by nature from the divine works of creation that there is a personal, eternal, and almighty God, the Creator, Preserver, and Ruler of the universe. This knowledge is derived also by observing God's continuous operation both in the realm of nature and in human history. Cf. Romans 1:20; Acts 14:15–17; Acts 17:26–28. In addition, the divine Law of God is written into the heart of all men. Thus God confronts man from within man's own self, manifesting Himself as the holy and righteous God, who demands and rewards the good and condemns and punishes the evil. Cf. Romans 1:32; 2:14, 15.

The natural knowledge of God is innate. It is furthermore increased by means of observing the realm of nature and by drawing conclusions from such observations. Because of this fact, all human beings are by nature religious.

RELIGION IN GENERAL

Religion cannot be easily defined, but the areas in which it operates are clear. Religion concerns itself with the relationship of man to his God and with the relationship of man to his fellow men. Heathen as well as Christians use the word *religion*. Since the heathen associate heathen concepts with this word and the Christians associate Christian concepts, it is impossible to formulate a definition of religion that would be comprehensive enough to include all forms of religion under one class as being acceptable to God.

In a general way religion may be described nevertheless. Broadly we may define religion as the beliefs, theories, or basic ideas by which man's life is lived. This generally includes an awareness, or a conviction, of the existence of a Supreme Being, which arouses in man a definite kind of behavior in accordance with these basic ideas.

Unfortunately, many people regard any religion that fits into the framework of such a definition as being acceptable to God. There is no justification for such a conclusion, because there is more to acceptable religion before God than is indicated in this definition. The definition may stand, however, when we consider religion in general.

How the Religious Practices
of Natural Man Develop

When we study the behavior of the human race throughout the world, we find that the religion of natural man, uninfluenced by Christ and the Gospel, will develop into different forms, ceremonies, practices, and beliefs. In some of these matters they may be similar, but in others they may differ greatly. It much depends on the intellectual development, human imagination, background, history, and environment of the individual. These matters determine the forms of religious obedience, reverence, and worship. In some religions self-denial and sacrifice are emphasized; in others self-chastisement, moral exercises, and ascetic discipline are more prominent. In some religions certain foods are forbidden; in others periodic pilgrimages to so-called sacred places and shrines are important. Certain matters may be a part of one man's religious practices, but are not so of another's. For example, ancestor worship is a major part of the religion in China. In India certain animals are regarded sacred by the adherents of the Hindu religion. Among Muslims the use of alcoholic beverages and tobacco is forbidden. Shamans are a part of religion in Africa.

NATURAL MAN'S CONCEPTION OF GOD

The religion of natural man may lead man to think of the Supreme Being in various ways. Some people believe in one god (monotheism), others in many gods (polytheism), and still others say that all is god (pantheism). Some maintain that the various ideas of God do not really matter, for they believe that different people may picture the same god in a different way and in a different manner, as though it were a matter of viewpoint. There are others who believe in a personal god who is regarded as not exerting any influence on men or on the world he has created (deism).

ARE ATHEISTS AND AGNOSTICS RELIGIOUS?

An atheist is one who denies the existence of God. An agnostic maintains that it is impossible to know God. On the surface it may appear as if atheists and agnostics are without religion, since they do not profess a religion nor are identified with organized religion. Yet they, too, have a religion; their life is guided by principles, loves, and moral convictions, and that is their religion. There isn't a man alive who doesn't worship something. If he does not worship the true God, he will worship something else, even if it be just his own proud self.

MAN'S NATURAL KNOWLEDGE OF GOD IS INADEQUATE

The religion of natural man has its basis in man's natural knowledge of God. The natural knowledge of God is insufficient to arrive at the right religion, as the Scriptures plainly teach. While natural man knows something about God (Romans 1:19, 20), he is, nevertheless, by nature spiritually dead (1 Corinthians 2:14), and therefore he cannot by his own reason or strength worship the true God. Natural man makes certain rational conclusions on the basis of his limited knowledge of God, and these conclusions prompt him to worship as he does. There is much perversion of the truth in the manner in which natural man practices his religion; whatever truth natural man possesses often is misinterpreted and misapplied. For example, God is pictured far beyond what the natural knowledge of God in man allows. Or man is credited with virtues and moral capacities contrary to the actual facts.

Furthermore, self-love is the motive of natural man in practicing his religion. In that respect all religions except Christianity are alike. While the forms and demonstrations of the religion of natural man may vary in different people and in different countries, the motive in all of them is the same. The motives are self-love and human pride, coupled with uncertainty, doubts, superstition, self-righteousness, and fear. In every instance natural man seeks to secure a right relationship with what he considers his highest good, or his God, by means of self-righteous efforts.

Whoever believes that man is reconciled to God, wholly or in part, through his own efforts is following the pagan conception of religion; he is a heathen, whether he lives among his own kind or in a so-called Christian country.

And yet it is a popular belief that all practices of religion are in one way or another facets of the true and right religion. This is a false assumption. No form of natural man's religion can ever be the right religion, because the element of truth in man's natural knowledge of God is perverted through man's rational conclusions.

SINCERITY IS NOT ENOUGH

We hear people say that if a man is sincere he will be saved. So any religion is believed to be good if its devotees are sincere. This is a common mistake among people. Sincerity of faith does not prove the truth of any religion. People can be sincerely wrong. "There is a way that seems right to a man, but its end is the way to death" (Proverbs 14:12). Sincerity is a necessary part of possessing the right religion but can never be a determining factor as to the correctness of the religion. This is so because sincerity is not a part of the religion itself but is a characteristic of the individual who possesses it.

Another prevalent false assumption is the idea that it does not make much difference what one believes, so long as one believes something about a God and about decency in human behavior. If it makes no difference what a man believes, then any belief or any kind of life may be acceptable on the grounds of religion. To maintain that any kind of faith will help and save is as foolish as to say that anything a person eats will provide nourishment.

Erroneous is also the idea that it does not matter what one believes, just so one lives right. To that we say: A way of living is a by-product of a way of believing. Jesus says: "In vain do they worship Me, teaching as doctrines the commandments of men" (Matthew 15:9).

RELIGIOUSLY, NATURAL MAN IS HELPLESS

It is a sad but true fact that natural man cannot arrive at the right religion by himself. He cannot by his own efforts know the true God and His revelation to man. He can no more contribute to such a knowledge by his own effort than he could have contributed to his own physical birth. "The natural person does not accept the things of the Spirit of God" (1 Corinthians 2:14). Basically the religion of all men by nature revolves around the works that men do, the sacrifices that men make, the righteousness that men according to their own standards endeavor to achieve, the denials that men practice. These bases are not the foundation of the Christian religion. Therefore, no one can by himself arrive at the right religion.

THE CORRECT BASIS OF FAITH IS ALL-IMPORTANT

The true and right religion depends on the correctness and truth of what we believe and in what we place our trust and confidence. If we believe the wrong things, our religion obviously will be false, no matter how sincere we may be. If we believe the right things, our religion will be right. Jesus made this clear in the Sermon on the Mount, when He spoke about the folly and disastrous results of building a house on sand and the wisdom and security of building a house on a rock. Cf. Matthew 7:24–27.

To be a Christian, one must build on the words of Christ. Jesus says: "If anyone loves Me, he will keep My word" (John 14:23).

CHRISTIANITY IS THE ONE TRUE RELIGION

Christianity is the true and right religion, because it is the one religion that comes to man from God, in whom it has its basis and foundation. It is the only religion revealed to man by God in His Word, and it is the only one bestowed upon man by God. Christianity is light from above. It is made known in the Bible, and it shows man that God has reconciled the sinful world to Himself through Jesus Christ, the Savior from sin for all mankind. "For God so loved the world, that He gave His only Son, that whoever believes in Him should not perish but have eternal life" (John 3:16). "The Christian religion is faith in the Gospel, that is, faith in the divine message that through the substitutionary satisfaction of Christ God is already reconciled to all men" (Francis Pieper, *Christian Dogmatics* [St. Louis: Concordia, 1950], 1:9). Cf. Galatians 2:16. Only the Christian religion reveals that God loves man. It shows the basis of this love as well as the demonstration of this love. According to the Christian religion it is not man, but God, who has done everything for man's salvation. Jesus Christ, the eternal Son of God, very God of very God, assumed the human nature into His divine being, lived for man on this earth, fulfilled for man the demands of God's Law, and paid for man's guilt of sin. In the Christian religion God assures man that He credits Christ's righteousness to man. This is wonderful news, so different from natural man's conception of getting right with God. It is called "the Gospel," which means "good news."

If we embrace the Christian religion, we are religious in the true and right manner, because we are right with God on God's terms.

CHAPTER 2

The Bible

The Holy Bible is the sourcebook of Christianity. In it God reveals the true religion to us. The Bible's own testimony bears witness to this truth: "These are written so that you may believe that Jesus is the Christ, the Son of God, and that by believing you may have life in His name" (John 20:31). "The sacred writings . . . are able to make you wise for salvation through faith in Christ Jesus. All Scripture is breathed out by God and profitable for teaching, for reproof, for correction, and for training in righteousness, that the man of God may be complete, equipped for every good work" (2 Timothy 3:15–17).

The Bible is its own best argument. It is self-authenticating; it testifies in its own behalf. The Scriptures not only tell us *that* they are the Word of God, but they also teach very clearly *why* they are the Word of God, namely, because they were inspired by God. Cf. 2 Timothy 3:16; 2 Peter 1:20, 21. This testimony of the Scriptures concerning themselves carries conviction, divine conviction. There is no outside evidence to compare with the Bible's internal proof. The Bible's sublime doctrines and moral precepts are evidence of the truth of the religion it proclaims. The Bible describes man in the true light and teaches that the salvation of man comes from God Himself.

How Are We to Consider Other So-called Sacred Books?

The so-called sacred books of world religions are not the revelation of God, as is evident from the teachings in these books. They are the outgrowth of man's imagination, and they present unwarranted and unjustified conclusions, which the limitations and inadequacy of man's natural knowledge do not permit. It has been said: "If they agree with the teachings of the Bible, they are unnecessary; if they do not agree with the teachings of the Bible, they must be rejected." This applies to the Qur'an of the Muslims, to the Book of Mormon of the Church of Jesus Christ of Latter-day Saints, to *Science and Health with Key to the Scriptures* of the Christian Scientists, and to all other man-made sacred books. They all teach that man must himself establish a right relationship with whatever force he considers God. The basic requirement in all of them is salvation by self-effort or the reconciliation of man to God by his own deeds. These books are of purely human origin and are not trustworthy in matters of faith and life. The Holy Bible admits of no other book of revelation from God.

FACTS ABOUT THE BIBLE

1. The *one theme* of the Bible is the salvation of sinful man by Jesus Christ. The theme of the Old Testament, which consists of thirty-nine books originally written in the Hebrew language, is salvation promised in the Messiah (Christ). The theme of the New Testament, which consists of twenty-seven books originally written in the Greek language, is salvation accomplished by Christ.

2. God is *the real Author* of the entire Bible. Bible means "book." It is a collection of sixty-six books which were written at various times between the years 1,500 BC and AD 100. Approximately forty writers participated in the writing. God, however, is the real Author because He inspired men to write the Bible. "Men spoke from God as they were carried along by the Holy Spirit" (2 Peter 1:21). "We impart this in words not taught by human wisdom but taught by the Spirit, interpreting spiritual truths to those who are spiritual" (1 Corinthians 2:13).

3. *Two fundamental doctrines,* which run practically through all the books of the Bible, are the Law and the Gospel. Both are the Word of God. They are radically different from each other as to content, purpose, and effect, and must be carefully distinguished from each other. The Law is that doctrine of the Bible in which God tells us how we are to be and what we are to do and not to do. The Gospel is that

doctrine of the Bible in which God tells us the good news of our salvation in Jesus Christ.

THE BIBLE IS GOD'S BOOK

The Bible claims for itself to be the Word of God. Of the Old Testament writings we read: "All Scripture is breathed out *by God*" (2 Timothy 3:16). Of the New Testament writers the apostle Paul says: "When you received the word of God, which you heard from us, you accepted it not as the word of men but as what it really is, *the word of God*" (1 Thessalonians 2:13). Jesus often referred His hearers to the Old Testament by introducing the reference with these words: "Have you not read?"

The strongest evidence of inspiration is within the Bible itself. First of all, Scripture says that God has inspired it. Furthermore, through the internal testimony of the Holy Spirit assurance is given that the Bible is God's inspired Word. Such assurance is entirely the work of God. Hence only the believer in the true God has discovered that the Bible is God's Word, for only by accepting its truths can man be certain that the Bible is God's Word.

There are also strong external evidences worthy of consideration when we speak of the Bible as the inspired revelation of God to man. One of these outside evidences is the power of the Bible to survive and to endure despite many efforts to destroy it. Another evidence is the power of the Bible to transform human lives. The blessed effects of the Bible on man are a powerful evidence; a book that is charged with the power of God must indeed be God's Book. The fulfillment of the Bible's prophecies, especially concerning Jesus Christ, also is strong evidence for the claim of the Bible to be the revelation of God.

MEANING OF INSPIRATION

The word *inspiration* means "a breathing in." "Divinely inspired" means "God-breathed." When we speak of the inspiration of the Bible by God, we mean that God gave the writers the impulse, or driving force, to write; that they wrote as God wanted them to write; and that they used the very forms of words God wanted used to express His divine thoughts. This is called "verbal inspiration." God moved the writers *when* they were to write, *what* they were to write, and *how* they were to write. Just how God inspired these writers, we are not told. While under the Spirit's direction, each writer was an individual who employed his individual talents and used expressions, general knowledge, and style peculiar to him.

How the Inspired Books Became Recognized

The thirty-nine books that constitute the Old Testament were in the days of Christ called "the Scripture"; they were commonly regarded by the Jewish nation as books having come from God. They called them "the Word of God." Jesus Himself so recognized them. He said: "You search the Scriptures because you think that in them you have eternal life; and it is they that bear witness about Me" (John 5:39).

If the Jews had been mistaken as to their canonical books (collection of books received as genuine and inspired Holy Scripture) or if they had falsified them, Christ would not have so unconditionally and without limitation pointed to the Scriptures in the hands of the Jews and asserted their inviolability. Cf. Luke 16:29; 24:44. Jewish tradition says that Ezra completed the collection. It is certain that from the time of the Maccabean persecution (ca. 165 BC) the Old Testament appears complete.

When the writings of the apostles and the evangelists appeared in the New Testament, they were gradually added to the Old Testament Scriptures and were held in the same sacred regard. They were accepted as the foundation of faith. In Ephesians 2:20 Paul says: "You are built upon the foundation of the apostles and prophets." Christ in His High Priestly Prayer (John 17:20) makes the Word of the apostles the basis of faith for the entire New Testament era. The apostles themselves point us to their Scriptures. Cf. 1 John 1:3, 4; 2 Thessalonians 2:15. Formal ratification of the twenty-seven books of the New Testament, as we now have them, took place at the Council of Carthage (AD 397); this merely expressed what already had become the unanimous judgment of the churches.

THE AUTHORITY OF THE BIBLE

The authority of the Bible lies in the supreme God, who stands behind every statement, doctrine, promise, and command of the Bible. "God spoke . . . by the prophets" (Hebrews 1:1). "The things I am writing to you are a command of the Lord" (1 Corinthians 14:37).

This authority cannot be superseded by any other. "I warn everyone who hears the words of the prophecy of this book: if anyone adds to them, God will add to him the plagues described in this book, and if anyone takes away from the words of the book of this prophecy, God will take away his share in the tree of life and in the holy city, which are described in this book" (Revelation 22:18–19). No one may add to the Bible or take away anything from it. We dare not corrupt the Word of God by putting our own meaning into the text, thereby endeavoring to make God say what we want Him to say. Whoever ignores, disregards, rejects, alters, or even only criticizes Holy Scripture, offends the very majesty of God, for he rebels against God's authority. Hence Christ's warning: "The word that I have spoken will judge him on the last day" (John 12:48).

The Bible is true in all things. Because God inspired the Bible to be written, every possibility of error, not only in the presentation of fundamental doctrines but also in such references as pertain to nature and history, was eliminated from the very outset. "Your Word is truth" (John 17:17).

MAY WE EXPECT NEW
AND ADDITIONAL REVELATIONS?

There is no need for new or for additional revelations from God. The Bible contains all the counsel of God. It is sufficient to teach us the path to salvation and to educate and train us in righteousness of life. There is no promise for additional revelations. On the contrary, God has directed and bound all Christians to the Last Day to the Word of the apostles and prophets. With this Word the period of divine revelation is closed. All Christians to the end of time come to faith through the Word of the apostles (John 17:20). The Church is built on the foundation of the apostles and prophets (Ephesians 2:20). The Bible lacks nothing to be supplied by further revelations or by new developments of doctrine.

WHAT DOES IT MEAN TO INTERPRET THE SCRIPTURES?

To interpret the Scriptures means that in our own words we explain and restate what the texts of the Bible actually mean and teach. A Scripture text can have but one divinely intended sense and meaning. We have a record of Bible interpretation in Luke 24:27, where Jesus expounded the Old Testament Scriptures to the two Emmaus disciples.

Christians have the right and the duty to show men what the Bible teaches and how *the Bible interprets itself.* However, every type and form of human authority over the Word is to be rejected.

In this connection we should bear in mind that not all that God ever said and did is recorded in the Bible. Neither have we in the Bible a complete revelation of all we should like to know of God's being, judgments, and purposes. However, all that is necessary and profitable for us to know, God has made known.

Holy Scripture contains matters that are incomprehensible to human reason. Examples include the doctrine of the Trinity, the doctrine of the Person of Christ, etc. What reason cannot comprehend, faith apprehends and takes "every thought captive to obey Christ" (2 Corinthians 10:5). When the message of salvation by Christ is preached to man, it is to him "a stumbling block . . . and folly" (1 Corinthians 1:23), for "the natural person does not accept the things of the Spirit of God, for they are folly to him" (1 Corinthians 2:14). No man can of himself arrive at the true interpretation of Holy Scripture. Without the illumination of the Holy Spirit not one letter of Scripture could be understood. It is by the power of God's Spirit that man becomes a believer. God convinces and assures man of His great love not by appealing to the natural powers of man, but by creating faith in the love of God by the preaching of the Gospel. Cf. Romans 10:17.

The lack of understanding many teachings of the Bible is due chiefly to a neglect of Bible reading and Bible study. If we read the Bible diligently, many teachings would become clearer to us. The occurrence of dark, difficult passages in Scripture should not disturb us but should lead us to a more diligent and prayerful study of Scripture.

THE PURPOSE OF THE BIBLE

God gave His Word to us to reveal Christ as the only Savior from sin. To that end the Law shows us our sins when our life is measured against its demands (Romans 3:20), and the Gospel leads us to trust in Jesus Christ as our Savior (2 Timothy 3:15; John 5:39; 20:31). The Bible furthermore reveals to us God's holy will pertaining to our life, namely, how we as His children should live (Psalms 119: 9, 105; 2 Timothy 3:16–17). The ultimate purpose of every doctrine of the Bible is that God may be glorified in all things.

Faith in God's promises brings the blessings we need and which God wants us to enjoy. We must learn and know what the Bible teaches if we are to arrive at the basis of a Christian faith and trust.

All are to read and study the Word of God. We are to meditate on what we have read and learned; by means of such meditation the meaning of the Scripture texts and truths unfolds itself more fully to our minds and sinks deeper into our hearts. We are to accept as true and to believe the Word of God, and we are to observe it in our life. We are also to teach those who do not have the Word of God, that they, too, may learn of salvation. Cf. Matthew 28:19–20.

There is a great advantage to memorizing certain Bible passages, for what we memorize and occasionally recall to our mind becomes a fixed treasure, not only of the mind but also of the heart. Knowing from memory some key passages will serve us well for comfort in trial and for strength in times of temptation.

The benefits of using the Bible are many and varied. First of all, the Bible makes us wise for salvation. A study of the Word keeps us in this wisdom. We all desire to be eternally saved. Second, the Bible guides us in the way we should live in this world. There should be in each one of us an earnest desire to live a God-pleasing life. A diligent and regular study of the Word is advocated by the Bible itself so that we may arrive at a deeper understanding of its teachings in order to apply them better to our life. We all should say with the psalmist (Psalm 19:10) that the Word of God is more to be desired "than gold, even much fine gold; sweeter also than honey and drippings of the honeycomb." Let us always remember how Christ commended Mary, who sat at His feet and listened to His Word.

The Bible is the sourcebook of all Christian doctrine. The Bible is given for admonition, for to recognize error we must test all religious teachings by the Word of God. We should use the Bible also that we may learn where and how our life may be in need of correction and improvement. For instruction and training in righteousness there is no book to compare with the Bible. We should use it also for comfort, for in this world of tribulation we need the assurance of God's protection and the promises of His grace and love.

THE BIBLE'S POWER

The Bible has the power to produce an effect. It can make an impression on man's heart. God operates with His Spirit through the Word of God on the heart of man. The Law produces a knowledge of sin and contrition of heart: "Through the law comes knowledge of sin" (Romans 3:20). The Gospel produces faith and hope: "For I am not ashamed of the gospel, for it is the power of God for salvation to everyone who believes" (Romans 1:16). Thus the Scriptures, the Holy Bible, are really able to make men wise for salvation through faith in Christ Jesus. In the Bible God reveals to us how a right relationship may be established and maintained between us and our Creator and Lord.

CHAPTER 3

The Lord Our God

Belief in the existence of a Supreme Being is universal among men. In every land and among all peoples there is a conviction that someone rules all and that man is accountable to him. Rarely do people deny the existence of a Higher Power because of a belief that He is nonexistent. Objections to the existence of God usually are the escape mechanisms of a bad conscience. No wonder that Psalm 14 insists that only a fool would say, "There is no God."

Since man by nature has a knowledge of the existence of God and realizes his accountability to Him, he will seek to identify this God. In so doing he invariably makes an idol. Man's natural knowledge of God and of His Law is incapable of leading man to know and to worship the true God. It is only by accepting the teaching of the Bible that man can arrive at a Christian knowledge of God, know and worship the one true God.

The gods whom natural man reveres are products of man's own imagination. In his imagination natural man has some very small ideas about God, and he looks for something to approximate these small ideas. Natural man is prone to cut down God to his own size to make Him compatible. He will fashion his god, or gods, after the pattern of men, imbuing him, or them, with some human and some superhuman qualities, as well as some human weaknesses. The ancient mythological figures of the Greek and Roman religions are examples of man's imagination of God.

Heathenism's Conception of God

The Chinese have an assortment of various deities whom they worship in various ways. Their religion is a mixture of three faiths: Confucianism, Taoism, and Buddhism. Among the various deities that the Chinese revere are little "kitchen gods." They are just paper images put on a shelf in the kitchen, the place where life could best be observed. At certain times the family must burn its little god so he can go back to heaven and report the sins of that household. In order to guarantee a favorable report, the Chinese will smear a little honey on the mouth of the paper image when the time comes to burn him, thus sweetening the report.

There are said to be more gods in India than people. The supreme god of Hinduism, the religion of India, is Brahma, who is never represented by any image because he is thought to be beyond the reach of thought and prayer. Vishnu and Siva, the highest-ranking gods after Brahma, are regarded as having material forms.

The Islamic god is Allah, who is considered an arbitrary ruler, bestowing his favors one day and his disfavors the next. Muslims think of God mainly in terms of power. They believe that Allah exercises his mercy and compassion by power rather than by love.

The absurdities of man's imagination of God in heathen lands may cause us to smile indulgently. Lest we think that people among us are much different, we ought to remember that there are many ignorant people in our own country who have some very quaint and vague ideas of their own about the Supreme Being. According to the attitude and belief of some, man may approach the stature of God, or be like God, by means of improving his behavior. Like the heathen religions, the Mormon religion, the religion of salvation by the Golden Rule, the Christian Science religion, and others maintain that man may by means of a good behavior attain divinity or "bring out the God" in him. The very fact that their religious practices are not as bold and crude as are the practices in heathen lands and that they frequently use Christian terminology and expressions does not eliminate some of the same basic false conceptions of God that we find among the heathen elsewhere.

Is It the Same God in Various Forms?

There are many who believe that different people think of the true God in different ways, and that all of them honor and revere the same true God. They feel that the Christian's God, the Hindu deities, Allah of the Muslims, and others, are to be regarded as the same Supreme Being under different names and conceptions and that each group merely considers the true God from a different point of view. Accordingly, one is not to say or to imply that anyone has a false god, for such an action would jeopardize all friendly relations with one's fellow men, a fact that would not be conducive to world brotherhood. Tacitly or openly Christians are sometimes criticized for going to foreign lands "to disturb and upset" the peoples of these lands in their particular beliefs. After all, they reason, whatever their concepts of God may be, they are but facets of the one true God. How wrong these assumptions are!

All Imaginary Gods Are Idols

Idol worship is found wherever man imagines God. We cannot imagine the true God. It is impossible to imagine anything that is purely and perfectly spiritual. Our limited mind simply cannot understand the boundless God. Any god who is the product of man's imagination must of necessity be an idol, a false god.

Nature Reveals Certain Things about God

Nature proves the existence of God to natural man. "For what can be known about God is plain to them, because God has shown it to them. For His invisible attributes, namely, His eternal power and divine nature, have been clearly perceived, ever since the creation of the world, in the things that have been made" (Romans 1:19–20). Neither the origin nor the continued existence of this world can be satisfactorily explained unless there is a Prime Cause that brought it into being and an almighty Power that sustains and governs it. "For every house is built by someone, but the builder of all things is God" (Hebrews 3:4). Nature does reveal God's power, wisdom, goodness, and unity, but it does not reveal *who* the true God is. The natural knowledge of God in man is limited to certain characteristics and qualities of God. God's power is evident when we study man, the animals, plant life, the solar system, the balance in nature, and so on. God's wisdom is evident when we study the functional design of muscle and bone structure in humans and animals, the power of seed to germinate, and the operation of the senses. God's goodness is evident not only in the bestowal of things necessary for life but also in the granting of many things that minister to our happiness, such as the fragrant flowers, the song of birds, and so forth. The amazing order and harmony to be found in nature is strong proof that one supreme mind planned it all and that one supreme will is ruling this world. Someone has claimed: "The existence of God could be proved statistically. Take the human body alone—the chance that all the functions of the individual would just happen is a statistical monstrosity."

When man on the basis of what he knows about God by nature tries to determine *who* God is, he will, in seeking to identify Him, invariably make an idol of Him, whether that be an imaginary being in his mind or some material object to which he attributes divinity. "For all the gods of the peoples are worthless idols, but the Lord made the heavens" (Psalm 96:5). The natural knowledge of God does not reveal to man the name of God, the will of God, or the gracious plan of salvation. It is therefore insufficient to meet man's needs.

CONSCIENCE PROVES THE EXISTENCE OF GOD

Man has proof for the existence of God in himself. His conscience, which holds him accountable for his deeds to a Power higher than himself, testifies to the existence of God. "Their conscience also bears witness, and their conflicting thoughts accuse or even excuse them" (Romans 2:15); the thoughts of men are either accusing or approving man's actions before a Being to whom they feel accountable. Conscience, however, does not reveal *who* the true God is.

THE BIBLE REVEALS THE TRUE GOD

The true God has more fully revealed Himself in the Bible. While nature and conscience tell us *that* there is a God, the Bible tells us *who* this God is. While nature and conscience reveal to us many of the qualities and characteristics of God, it is the Bible that not only emphasizes and elaborates upon them but also tells us of God's love and grace in Christ and makes known to us the salvation that God has prepared for us.

We need to know God. We need not merely to know facts about Him and His character, but we need an insight into His design toward us and His will for us. Such knowledge of God gives us not merely items to be stored up in the memory but the supply of the very life of God, which alone makes us blessed. "And this is eternal life, that they know You the only true God, and Jesus Christ whom You have sent" (John 17:3).

The Bible teaches that God is a personal being, absolute and supreme (Exodus 3:14), that He is a Spirit (John 4:24), without a material nature, and that He is and subsists of and by Himself (Isaiah 44:6; John 5:26). Whenever the Bible speaks of God as though He were a human being, having arms, hands, fingers, face, it is using figurative language to adapt the concept of God to our finite mind, which cannot conceive and realize the spiritual nature of the infinite God.

ATTRIBUTES, OR CHARACTERISTICS, OF GOD

God is one. God is in a class by Himself. There can be no other God besides Him. "I am the LORD, and there is no other, besides Me there is no God" (Isaiah 45:5). "There is no God but one" (1 Corinthians 8:4). "The LORD our God, the LORD is one" (Deuteronomy 6:4). Therefore: "You shall have no other gods before Me" (Exodus 20:3) and "You shall worship the Lord your God and Him only shall you serve" (Matthew 4:10). The doctrine of the oneness of God is important. If He blesses us, no other god can curse us. "If God is for us, who can be against us?" (Romans 8:31). But if He is turned against us, "there is none to deliver out of Your [God's] hand" (Job 10:7).

God is indivisible. He is not compounded of parts or elements. God is a simple, indivisible essence. "I AM WHO I AM" (Exodus 3:14).

God is unchangeable. He is unchangeable in His essence. In Psalm 102:26–27 the psalmist brings into the sharpest contrast the change and decay to which all creatures are heirs and the immutability of God: "They will perish, but You will remain . . . they will pass away, but You are the same, and Your years have no end." God is what He is, what He always was, and what He always will be. Cf. Malachi 3:6. God is immutable also in all His attributes; for example, His kindness (Isaiah 54:10), His wrath (John 3:36), and His will (Proverbs 19:21). The Bible draws a twofold lesson from God's immutability: (1) to warn the wicked, because God's wrath is unchangeable (Mark 9:48); (2) to comfort the pious, because God's grace can never depart (Isaiah 54:10).

God is infinite. He is not limited by space and confined to it. He is present everywhere. "Behold, heaven and the highest heaven cannot contain You" (1 Kings 8:27). "Yet He is actually not far from each one of us, for 'In Him we live and move and have our being' " (Acts 17:27–28). "Can a man hide himself in secret places so that I cannot see him? declares the LORD. Do I not fill heaven and earth? declares the LORD" (Jeremiah 23:24).

This doctrine is of great comfort to us, for it means that God's blessings are as near as He is and that in the hour of need we should have no fear. It also is a warning to us, for it also means that we cannot hide from Him when we are disobedient and perverse.

God is eternal. He is not limited by time. "From everlasting to everlasting You are God" (Psalm 90:2). With God there is neither past nor future but one everlasting present. "With the Lord one day is as a thousand years, and a thousand years as one day" (2 Peter 3:8). This fact gives us comfort, for only then can His blessings continue to be upon us. How hopeless to believe in a God whose existence might terminate.

God is a living, intelligent, active being. "But the LORD is the true God, He is the living God" (Jeremiah 10:10). "How unsearchable are His judgments and how inscrutable His ways" (Romans 11:33). God is constantly active in preserving and governing the world. "In Him we live and move and have our being" (Acts 17:28). This means for us that God is the source of all life and activity in the world. It is a comfort to all Christians, for they have their "hope set on the living God" (1 Timothy 4:10). It is a warning to all unbelievers, for "it is a fearful thing to fall into the hands of the living God" (Hebrews 10:31).

God knows all things; He is omniscient. "The LORD is a God of knowledge" (1 Samuel 2:3). "God is greater than our heart, and He knows everything" (1 John 3:20). "The eyes of the LORD are in every place, keeping watch on the evil and the good" (Proverbs 15:3). This serves as a warning that we realize we cannot hide anything from Him. "Whoever conceals his transgressions will not prosper" (Proverbs 28:13). It serves as a comfort to realize that God knows our sorrows and troubles and is ready to help us. The Lord says: "But this is the one to whom I will look: he who is humble and contrite in spirit and trembles at My word" (Isaiah 66:2).

God is wise. "With God are wisdom and might; He has counsel and understanding" (Job 12:13). The wisdom of God is manifest in nature. It is evident especially in the work of our redemption and salvation. The wisdom of God far surpasses the understanding of man. "Oh, the depth of the riches and wisdom and knowledge of God" (Romans 11:33). The wisdom of God means to us that God knows in every case what to do and how to do it, how to dispose and ordain all causes and effects for the attainment of His purposes. God has all the answers for all our problems, and whatever He ordains is good.

God has a will. God consciously prompts His own acts and is intent upon the execution of His purposes. "My counsel shall stand, and I will accomplish all My purpose . . . I have spoken, and I will bring it to pass; I have purposed, and I will do it" (Isaiah 46:10–11). God has, however, not made known to us many of the things in His mind. The revealed holy will of God is the Law, or the Ten Commandments, wherein God tells us what to do and not to do, and how we are to be and not to be. The gracious will of God is the Gospel, wherein God tells us that He will have all men to be saved and to come unto the knowledge of the truth; this is the will mentioned in the Lord's Prayer: "Thy will be done on earth as it is in heaven."

God is holy. He is opposed to and abhors every type of iniquity and sin. "Holy, holy, holy is the LORD of hosts; the whole earth is full of His glory" (Isaiah 6:3). "For You are not a God who delights in wickedness; evil may not dwell with You" (Psalm 5:4).

God is just and righteous. Whatever God does is right. He is outside of and above all law. Whatever He pleases to do or not to do is of itself right and just. "A God of faithfulness and without iniquity, just and upright is He" (Deuteronomy 32:4). God's dealings at times appear unjust to man because man judges them by human standards. We should unquestionably accept them as God's wise ways. "For My thoughts are not your thoughts, neither are your ways My ways, declares the LORD. For as the heavens are higher than the earth, so are My ways higher than your ways and My thoughts than your thoughts" (Isaiah 55:8–9). Whatever God ordains is good and right.

God is truthful. His words and promises truly express His intentions and will. "For the word of the LORD is upright, and all His work is done in faithfulness" (Psalm 33:4). "God . . . never lies" (Titus 1:2). The absolute truthfulness of God pertains to all that is written in His Word. "Your Word is truth" (John 17:17). God's promises do not fail.

God is almighty; He is omnipotent. He possesses all power, and He can do and does whatever He purposes to do. "He does all that He pleases" (Psalm 115:3). The power of God never exhausts itself. "For nothing will be impossible with God" (Luke 1:37). This does not mean that God could do anything that would involve a contradiction of and disagreement with Himself. God can use His power directly, or He can use it mediately, through natural means, for example, when He sustains us through food. To know that God is able to do exceedingly above all that we might ask or think is of great comfort to every believer in Christ. There is no problem so great, no need so desperate, no burden so heavy that our God cannot resolve it for us.

God is good. In Himself He is absolutely good; there is no fault or defect in Him; He is perfect in every respect. "There is only one who is good" (Matthew 19:17). God is good and kind to His creatures; He is benevolent and desires to bless them. "The LORD is good to all, and His mercy is over all that He has made" (Psalm 145:9). God is love, desirous of bringing the lost children of men back into communion with Himself. "I have loved you with an everlasting love; therefore I have continued My faithfulness to you" (Jeremiah 31:3). "For God so loved the world, that He gave His only Son, that whoever believes in Him should not perish but have eternal life" (John 3:16). God is merciful; He has compassion with the afflicted and bestows His blessings upon them. God is gracious, since He offers and confers His blessings regardless of the merits or demerits of the objects of His benevolence. God is long-suffering, slow to anger. "The LORD, the LORD, a God merciful and gracious, slow to anger, and abounding in steadfast love and faithfulness, keeping steadfast love for thousands, forgiving iniquity and transgression and sin" (Exodus 34:6–7). The goodness of God is the very heart of God. Because of the goodness of God, all other attributes of God are used in our interest and comfort us. The power of God, the wisdom of God, and all other attributes of God are very comforting to us only because God is good and because He loves us.

THE TRIUNE GOD

The Bible teaches that the true God is one undivided and indivisible essence, in which there are three distinct persons, which are the Father, the Son, and the Holy Spirit. The words *triune* or *Trinity* mean "three in one." The Bible teaches a strict monotheism, that there is but one God. But it also teaches that there is a trinity in this unity. In Matthew 3:16–17 the three persons of the Holy Trinity are mentioned. In Matthew 28:19 we read: "Go therefore and make disciples of all nations, baptizing them in the name of the Father and of the Son and of the Holy Spirit."

The Bible tells us that each of the three persons of the Trinity is to be acknowledged as God; but it also tells us that these three persons constitute one God only. The Father is true God. "Yet for us there is one God, the Father, from whom are all things and for whom we exist" (1 Corinthians 8:6). Jesus Christ, the Son, is true God. In 1 John 5:20, it says that Jesus "is the true God and eternal life." In Romans 9:5, it is stated that Jesus "is God over all, blessed forever." The Holy Spirit is true God. In Acts 5:3–4, the Holy Spirit is called God, and in

1 Corinthians 3:16, Christians are called "the temple of God" because the Holy Spirit dwells in them.

We Cannot Understand How God Is

The doctrine of the Trinity can be understood and proved only from the Word of God. We can therefore define God to the extent He has told us what He is like. Only God knows God; He dwells "in unapproachable light" (1 Timothy 6:16). "No one has ever seen God" (John 1:18). But God revealed Himself to man so that man can, in a measure, know God. He reveals Himself to man in the realm of nature, which is the source of the natural knowledge of God. He reveals Himself in the Word, which is the source of the saving knowledge of God. "The only God, who is at the Father's side, He has made Him known" (John 1:18). Only Christians can intelligently speak of what the Godhead essentially is, of His outward manifestation in His creatures and of His will toward men concerning their salvation. All this is told them by the Holy Spirit, who reveals and proclaims it through the Word.

The divine essence and the divine attributes of God are absolutely identical, because God is infinite and above space (1 Kings 8:27) and above time (Psalm 90:2, 4). Our finite human reason cannot comprehend the infinite, absolute, and uncompounded God. When God teaches us in His Word to distinguish between God's essence and His attributes, He adopts our way of thinking and accommodates Himself to the laws of human thought processes or logic. Our knowledge of God is subject to limitations which cannot define God. Adam's natural knowledge of God, even during his state of perfection, had sharp limitations. The Christian's renewed knowledge by means of his conversion likewise has limitations. Much of God remains inscrutable to the senses and comprehension of man. With Zophar we exclaim: "Can you find out the deep things of God? Can you find out the limit of the Almighty?" (Job 11:7). And the Scriptures echo the inscrutability of God (Ecclesiastes 8:17; Isaiah 40:28; Romans 11:33–34). Our finite and imperfect reason cannot comprehend the infinite perfection of God.

St. Augustine one morning was walking along the seashore, meditating on the doctrine of the Holy Trinity. "Three persons in one divine essence," mused he, "equal in divine power, glory, and majesty, yet but one God. How can that be?" While in vain he was trying to search the mystery of the Godhead, he noticed a little child playing on the shore. With a colored shell in its hand the child scooped a hole into the sand, then ran to the waves, filled the shell with water, came back and emptied its contents into the hole. "What are you trying to do?" asked Augustine. "I am trying to pour the sea into this hole," replied the child. "Oh," thought Augustine, "that is exactly what I have been trying to do, standing on the shore of time by the ocean of the eternal and infinite Godhead and attempting to grasp it with my finite mind."

THE DOCTRINE OF THE TRINITY IS ESSENTIAL

The doctrine of the Trinity is absolutely essential to the Christian religion. The man who rejects this doctrine cannot be considered a Christian. Many believe themselves to be Christians because they believe in a god but not in the triune God. To them Christ is but a model man, after whom we are to fashion our life in order to be saved. Such people are not Christian, because they do not accept the Bible's teachings about God, the triune God, and therefore they also do not accept the doctrine of redemption and salvation as taught in the Bible.

Faith in the true God means more than accepting the bare teaching of three persons in one divine essence. It includes reliance on and confidence in the saving work of the Trinity, how the Father sent Jesus, the Son, into the world to redeem sinful mankind by His blameless life and by His innocent suffering and death, and how the Holy Spirit brings us into the Christian faith and into communion with God. "All may honor the Son, just as they honor the Father. Whoever does not honor the Son does not honor the Father who sent Him. Truly, truly, I say to you, whoever hears My word and believes Him who sent Me has eternal life. He does not come into judgment, but has passed from death to life" (John 5:23–24). And Jesus said, "And I will ask the Father, and He will give you another Helper [the

Holy Spirit], to be with you forever, even the Spirit of truth, whom the world cannot receive, because it neither sees Him nor knows Him. You know Him, for He dwells with you and will be in you" (John 14:16–17). To acknowledge God as our Father and Jesus Christ as our Savior, we need the indwelling of the Holy Spirit. The doctrine of the Holy Trinity is a fundamental article of our Christian faith.

CHAPTER 4

Created and Preserved by God

We are living in a wonderful world, filled with animate and inanimate objects to arouse our interest and to stir our imagination. Men and women have sought the answer to questions pertaining to the origin, development, and preservation of this material world. They have dug into the earth, surveyed the earth strata, analyzed the state of civilization among the earth's peoples, made comparisons of the anatomy of plant life, of animal, and of man. The result of their investigation has been a vast array of theories. The Bible account of creation leaves no room for any evolutionary theory of creation. Wherever the almighty God stands behind a record, all accounts at variance with His record necessarily must be wrong.

God's Own Record of Creation

In Genesis, chapters 1 and 2, we have God's own record of His own work. Very simply and factually the Bible reports: "In the beginning, God created the heavens and the earth" (Genesis 1:1). And in the very last book of the Bible we read: "Worthy are You, our Lord and God, to receive glory and honor and power, for You created all things, and by Your will they existed and were created" (Revelation 4:11). The creation was a free and voluntary act of God. The Bible speaks of the creation of the world in which we now live. Whether God created or is still creating other worlds is an idle question.

THE MEANING OF CREATION

By the word *create* the Bible means that God brought into being or caused to exist. God created the world out of nothing. There was no substance of any kind that God used in forming the universe.

God alone existed before the creation. "He is before all things, and in Him all things hold together" (Colossians 1:17). "Before the mountains were brought forth, or ever You had formed the earth and the world, from everlasting to everlasting You are God" (Psalm 90:2). By His almighty power God called all things into being.

IS CREATION COMPATIBLE WITH HUMAN REASONING?

The existence of the world, its creation and preservation, is not a matter of conjecture or of idle guesswork with the Christian. Nor is it a matter of reasonable consideration. It is a matter of faith in God's record of creation. The Christian does not seek to make the Genesis account of creation compatible with human reasoning, but simply accepts God's account—that it was the almighty word of God that called things into being out of nothing and created something that was not there before. "By faith we understand that the universe was created by the word of God, so that what is seen was not made out of things that are visible" (Hebrews 11:3).

PERIOD OF CREATION

The almighty God did not need any period of time, long or short, to complete His creative work. He might have created the entire world, as it now is, in the twinkling of an eye. He might have allowed it to develop over long periods of time. But God definitely tells us that He began and completed the work of creation in six consecutive days. The expression "evening and morning" in the Genesis account marks the days of creation as ordinary days. Beginning with the fourth day (Genesis 1:14–19), the present solar system was put into operation, the sun to rule the day and the moon the night.

On the first day God created the crude material: heaven and earth, water, and elemental light. Cf. Genesis 1:1–5.

On the second day God made the firmament to divide the waters below from the waters above the firmament. Cf. Genesis 1:6–8.

On the third day God separated the land from the sea and caused the land to bring forth grass, the herb yielding seed and the tree yielding fruit, whose seed was in itself. Cf. Genesis 1:9–13.

On the fourth day God made the sun, the moon, and the numerous stars, placing them in the canopy of heaven. They became the bearers of light which God created on the first day. The elemental light was now concentrated into these heavenly luminaries. Their purpose is to give light on earth and to divide time into days, seasons, and years. Cf. Genesis 1:14–19.

On the fifth day God called forth numerous and various species of fish, marine animals, and birds, and, blessing them, enabled them to multiply on earth. Cf. Genesis 1:20–23.

On the sixth day God commanded the earth to bring forth all manner of living creatures, cattle and beasts and creeping things, each after his kind, bestowing on them the blessing to be able to reproduce themselves. Finally God formed the most noble creature for whose benefit, use, and enjoyment He had produced all the rest; God made man. Cf. Genesis 1:24–28.

"And on the seventh day God finished His work that He had done, and He rested on the seventh day from all His work that He had done" (Genesis 2:2). This simply means that God ceased creating new and additional things.

THE CREATION OF MAN

The details of the creation of man mark him as the chief and foremost of all visible creatures. Not only did God, as it were, take counsel with Himself, but He fashioned the body of a mature man, Adam, from the dust of the ground, breathed into his nostrils the breath of life (Genesis 2:7), gave him a rational soul and a conscience, and created him in His own image. On the same day God made one mature woman, Eve, of a rib that He had taken from Adam (Genesis

2:21–22). Man was created to rule in God's stead over the world. God gave him dominion over every living thing that moved on the earth (Genesis 1:28).

Man consists of body and soul in one complete person (Genesis 2:7; Ecclesiastes 12:7). The body of man is made of the dust of the ground (Genesis 2:7), to which it will revert in time of death (3:19). The soul of man is not a material but an immortal, living, spiritual essence, the composition and structure of which we do not understand. It dwells in the body (Acts 20:10), gives life to the body, and makes use of the body's several members according to the purpose for which they were designed. The interrelation and interaction of soul and body are a profound mystery.

Man can reason, think, and learn. He is a moral creature, who has some knowledge of God and His Law (Genesis 2:16–17). He has a conscience, which urges him to comply with this Law and holds him guilty if he fails to do so.

Conscience

Conscience is a powerful force and monitor in man's life, which urges him to do or not to do what he himself believes to be right or wrong. Conscience is not acquired after birth but is a part of humanity by nature. It distinguishes human beings from the beast of the field. It is not the same as humanity's moral convictions; neither is it to be identified with natural knowledge of the Law. Conscience is like a judge, and the natural knowledge of right and wrong is the law according to which it judges. Conscience does not examine the correctness of our convictions; whatever our convictions may be, conscience simply urges us to comply with them in our lives and judges our actions according to them. Conscience, therefore, may be defined as "a feeling of compulsion," whereby we feel we ought to do what we believe to be right, and we ought to avoid what we believe to be wrong. Conscience is active only when our moral convictions are put to a test; then it obligates us to comply with these convictions. So conscience either approves what we have done, or it holds us guilty whenever we fail.

While our conscience must not be ignored, it is, in itself, not an infallible guide of conduct; for if conscience is controlled by a wrong rule or law, it will urge us to comply with that wrong rule. The apostle Paul as a persecutor of the Christians obeyed his conscience, which was controlled by the false conviction that he was serving God by persecuting them. Later, as a follower of Christ, he also followed his conscience, which then was controlled by an enlightened understanding and knowledge of what God demanded of him. There is really no such thing as an erring conscience or a doubting conscience; any error lies in man's convictions, and any doubt lies in the understanding. Conscience, therefore, is not an infallible guide; it depends on the correctness of our convictions, if our conscience is to urge us to do right.

Adam and Eve were created with a perfect understanding of God's will and with a conscience which reacted to that understanding. Yet it was possible for them to violate their conscience, because they had a free will. By creation, in their state of perfection, they possessed a free will either to resist or to yield to temptation. This is evident from the fact that God placed the tree of the knowledge of good and evil in the Garden of Eden and that He gave Adam and Eve definite instructions regarding the use of that tree; it was placed by God as a test of man's obedience to the known will of God. Cf. Genesis 2:17.

God created human beings to procreate. In the beginning God made one man and one woman and joined them in wedlock to be one flesh (Genesis 2:18, 21–24), that they should be fruitful and multiply and thus replenish the earth (1:27–28). God "made from one man every nation of mankind to live on all the face of the earth" (Acts 17:26).

THE PRIMEVAL STATE OF MAN

In his original state man was good in every respect. The physical condition of his body was perfect (Genesis 2:17; Romans 5:12). The rational powers of his soul were perfect. The spiritual relation of man to God was perfect; the image of God, in which man was created, was a spiritual likeness to God, had its seat in man's soul, and was reflected in his life. The moral law was given by God to man at the time of man's creation. God created Adam and Eve with a natural knowledge of the law, and this knowledge was perfect. Cf. Genesis 1:26; 2:16–17; 3:3. Our first parents instinctively knew what was right and what was wrong. In Ecclesiastes 7:29, we read: "See, this alone I found, that God made man upright, but they have sought out many schemes." All that is excellent in man is from God; his sinfulness and folly are his own. Christians are urged to behave like our first parents in their perfection. Cf. Colossians 3:10; Ephesians 4:24. The mutual relation between the man and the woman was ideal, each fully understanding and observing the duties and restrictions of his position, and each regarding the other as a precious gift of their Creator. The relation of man to the other creatures on earth was one of dominion and rule. Cf. Genesis 1:28–29; 2:15.

The Angels,
the Foremost Invisible Creatures

Foremost of the invisible creatures of God are the angels. We find no evidence of their existence in nature, for we do not sense any contact with them. We do know from the Bible that angels exist. Cf. Daniel 7:10; Psalm 103:20–21; Luke 2:13. The word *angel* means "messenger."

Angels are distinct spiritual beings (Psalm 104:4; Hebrews 1:14), who have no bodies in which they live but are complete in their spiritual nature. They are personal beings (Luke 1:19), who are conscious of their existence and personality. They are rational beings (Luke 15:10), possessing knowledge and wisdom (2 Samuel 14:20) and strength (Psalm 103:20), but are neither almighty nor do they possess all knowledge (Mark 13:32). Angels are sexless and do not marry and propagate their kind (Matthew 22:30). They are immortal (Luke 20:36).

Originally all angels were good. Many of them still are. They are holy (Matthew 25:31; Luke 9:26) and enjoy everlasting bliss and communion with God (Matthew 18:10), which consists of willing and joyful service to God. They praise God (Luke 2:13–14) and carry out

His commands (Psalm 103:20–21). They are employed to minister to all that fear God and walk in His ways (Psalm 34:7; 91:11) and are the guardians especially of the children (Matthew 18:10). There are a great number of good angels (Luke 2:13; Daniel 7:10), and they possess great power (Psalm 103:20).

It is most comforting for Christians to know that the angels of God watch over them (Psalm 91:11–12), and we should strive to live as God's children that we never forfeit the protection of these heavenly messengers, so that we may always have the right and privilege to pray: "Let Your holy angel be with me that the evil foe may have no power over me!" However, we are not to worship angels (Colossians 2:18; Revelation 22:8–9).

Some of the good angels became evil. They sinned (2 Peter 2:4; John 8:44; Jude 6) by voluntary abuse of their will. We do not know the nature of their sin or the date of their fall; possibly it was after the sixth day of creation and before the devil tempted our first parents. The evil angels, whose leader is Satan (Matthew 25:41; Revelation 12:9), are now forever rejected and will never return to God (Matthew 25:41). There are many evil angels (Mark 5:9), and they are powerful (Ephesians 6:12). The evil angels are utterly depraved, perverted, and wicked (Mark 1:23). They are adversaries of God and man and seek to destroy the works of God and to counteract God's gracious purposes with man, as we see from the temptation in the Garden of Eden (Genesis 3) and from the temptation of Christ (Matthew 4:1–11). But they shall not prevail against the Church of Jesus (Matthew 16:18; Romans 16:20). They must serve the purposes of God in chastising the pious, as God permitted them to do to Job, and in punishing the wicked (Psalm 78:49).

GOD STILL RULES THE WORLD

God is constantly and actively present with all things He has made, keeping and sustaining, directing and governing them. "For by Him all things were created . . . and in Him all things hold together" (Colossians 1:16–17). God "upholds the universe by the word of His power" (Hebrews 1:3).

God employs His creatures as means to give support and sustenance to one another. The herb of the field and the fruit of the tree were given man "for food" (Genesis 1:29). After the fall into sin this was expanded so as to include the flesh of animals. Cf. Genesis 9:3; Psalm 104:14–15. The entire creation is a wonderful workshop of God, in which all things are integrated for mutual service.

The Laws of Nature Are Subject to God

God uses the forces and laws of nature in His work of preservation. He is the Prime Cause. This fact is of real significance to us, for it indicates God's personal interest in us, strengthens in us the assurance that God can easily make all things serve our needs, and makes secure for us the basis for our prayers. "For He makes His sun rise on the evil and on the good, and sends rain on the just and on the unjust" (Matthew 5:45). "You cause the grass to grow for the livestock and plants for man to cultivate, that he [man] may bring forth food from the earth" (Psalm 104:14). No creature, animate or inanimate, acts independently of God, even as no creature exists independently of God. "Are not two sparrows sold for a penny? And not one of them will fall to the ground apart from your Father. But even the hairs of your head are all numbered" (Matthew 10:29–30).

The Government of God

God most excellently orders, regulates, and directs the affairs and actions of all creatures according to His wisdom, justice, and goodness for the glory of His name and for the welfare of man. To that end God controls the laws of nature (Genesis 8:22; Matthew 5:45; Acts 14:17), governs the destiny of nations (history of Israel), and orders the lives of individuals (Proverbs 16:9; Psalm 33:13–15)

Although God at times permits evil to happen and men to walk in their perverse ways (Psalm 81:12; Acts 14:16; Romans 1:24), He does control the evil in the world (Acts 9; Psalm 33:10; 91:10–12; Genesis 50:20). God determines the length to which wicked men go, but He does not will the evil; and He so regulates and limits the results of evil actions that all things must in the end work out for the good of His children. Cf. Romans 8:28.

God is not responsible for man's evil deeds. He has no pleasure in wickedness. "Let no one say when he is tempted, 'I am being tempted by God,' for God cannot be tempted with evil, and He Himself tempts no one. But each person is tempted when he is lured and enticed by his own desire" (James 1:13–14).

FATALISM IS NOT IN ACCORD WITH SCRIPTURE

Fatalism is the doctrine that all events are determined by necessity, or fate, and that nothing can be done about it. Fatalists have an attitude of resignation, which is not Christian. What light do the Scriptures shed on fatalism?

Scriptures do teach that all things occur according to the determinate counsel of God. For example, from Acts 4:27–28 and Matthew 26:54 we learn that Christ's betrayal, arraignment, and death were determined beforehand by God. Scripture tells us that God calls members into the Christian Church (1 Peter 2:9; 2 Timothy 1:9; 2 Thessalonians 2:14; Acts 2:47). So all events in life happen as they are decreed by God. Everyone must say: "My times are in Your hand" (Psalm 31:15). As far as God is concerned, there are no surprises in the life of His creatures. No sparrow falls to the ground without His will. The hairs of our head are numbered. According to the law of divine providence, which rules all things, it is correct to say that all things happen of necessity, because they are determined by God.

This raises questions. Must all events in life occur as they do? Could they happen otherwise if we did certain things? If our life is fixed, can we do anything to lengthen or shorten it and thus cause God's plans to be changed? How useful is man's planning for life and living? The fatalist is resigned to the fact that, as to the final outcome, it is futile to do anything in the face of a predetermined situation. This is an anti-Christian attitude, since it denies the possibility of any personal relation with God, and it also disregards other directives of God.

The same Scriptures which teach that all things are determined by God also teach that we in all our ways are to make diligent use of the various means God has given us for a life of well-being.

For example, Jesus by means of confession to the truth sought to keep Pilate from pronouncing an unjust sentence (John 19:11–12). By declaring His innocence, Christ withstood His enemies. God has us use the Means of Grace to win the world for Christ. We are to use whatever means God has given us to maintain our life and well-being. In sickness we should seek medical advice and use medication. In building the Christian life, we should use the Means of Grace. We are not to disregard the means for living because we know that God has determined all things to occur as they do.

From God's standpoint all is determined, but from the human standpoint we are to use whatever means God has given us to make a life. These two matters are not at all contradictory, even though the first proposition appears to rule out the second. Fatalism, which emphasizes the first and disregards the importance of the second proposition, is an attitude that is contrary to the directives and teachings of Scripture.

God's Ultimate Purpose of the Creation

While the entire creation is a manifestation of God's almighty power and wisdom, and while things are in themselves good and intended for the use and benefit of man, the ultimate purpose of creation is the glory of God. "Worthy are You, our Lord and God, to receive glory and honor and power, for You created all things, and by Your will they existed and were created" (Revelation 4:11).

How fitting that the writer in Psalm 148 calls upon all creatures to praise God!

The Prevailing Note of the Christian Life

With the Christian life there is but one theme. Our life should ever have the praise of God as its prevailing note. That is the strain of the psalmist in writing: "Let everything that has breath praise the LORD" (Psalm 150:6). Let life be charged and crowned with praise!

Our life—a psalm, a psalm of praise! That is the life of holy fragrance, well-pleasing to God.

First we ought to praise God for what He is *in Himself.* In Psalm 89:6 we read: "For who in the skies can be compared to the LORD? Who among the heavenly beings is like the LORD?"

The majesty of God alone is deserving of our sacrifice of praise. God is our Creator and Lord.

The number and preciousness of God's blessings upon us are the second reason for praising God. The blessings of body and soul from God are bountiful. God deserves unlimited praise from us because of them. With the psalmist every Christian will exclaim: "What shall I render to the LORD for all His benefits to me? . . . I will pay my vows to the LORD in the presence of all His people" (Psalm 116:12, 14).

CHAPTER 5

Sin, the Great Despoiler

The marvelous world in which we live has been ruined by sin. While the world is steeped in sin, the word *sin* is not popular. People would rather hear nothing about it or would rather make light of it.

DEFINITION OF SIN

Sin is doing what God forbids, or failing to do what He commands. It is rebellion against God. Since the moral law tells us what God wants us to do and not to do, "sin is lawlessness" (1 John 3:4). Sin is not just something that everybody has to go through in the business of growing up. Every transgression of the Law, great or small, known or unknown, in thought, word, and deed, is sin. An act that is performed without a sense of moral responsibility remains a sin if it is contrary to God's will. The question of whether or not anything is sin is not determined by what we or others think about it but is determined by the requirements of the Law of God. On the other hand, the views and opinions of men cannot make anything sin if it is not contrary to the will of God. Sin is never all right. Sin is a condition as well as an act. God never made light of sin, and we, too, should not.

ORIGIN OF SIN

Sin did not originate with God or with man. The devil was the first to sin, and he brought sin into the world. "The devil has been sinning from the beginning" (1 John 3:8); the very first recorded sin was caused by the devil. Even before that time he had rebelled against God. Although created good and perfect (2 Peter 2:4; John 8:44), the devil and other angels transgressed some commandment of God, and thus evil originated. We do not know what particular sin they committed, but we do know that they rebelled against God.

THE DEVIL TEMPTED ADAM AND EVE

Man was tempted by the devil. Cf. Genesis 3:1–7. Of their own free will Adam and Eve yielded to the temptation of Satan and were, therefore, responsible for their transgression. It was an entirely voluntary act on the part of man.

Humanity's original state of innocence came to an end when Adam and Eve fell into sin. By transgressing one positive and express commandment, namely, not to eat from a certain tree in the Garden of Eden, Adam and Eve transgressed the whole Law (James 2:10), because thereby they broke through the restraint of the entire moral law, within which God wanted them to live.

The immediate result of man's fall into sin was the loss of the image of God. Having sinned, man was no longer holy; being guilty, he was no longer innocent. Man's holy relation to God ceased (Genesis 3:8, 10–12; Ephesians 2:1). So man came under the just wrath and curse of God. "But of the tree of the knowledge of good and evil you shall not eat, for in the day that you eat of it you shall surely die" (Genesis 2:17).

There were further consequences of man's fall into sin. Man's moral relation to his neighbor changed, as witnessed by the murder of Abel by Cain. Man lost his love for his neighbor and became selfish. The humanity's dominion over nature became curtailed. Life became a fierce battle. All created things were made subject to vanity and corruption (Romans 8:20–22). The mental faculties of man lost their original perfection, and physically man became weakened. Cf. Genesis 3:16–19, 21; Romans 5:12; 6:23. Man became mortal.

WE INHERITED ADAM'S TOTAL CORRUPTION

By the disobedience of our first parents sin entered into the world, and through sin misery, suffering, and death came upon all men. "Therefore, just as sin came into the world through one man, and death through sin, . . . so death spread to all men because all sinned" (Romans 5:12). All mankind has inherited from Adam a total corruption of the whole human nature. This total corruption passes on from parents to children. This inherited corruption is called "the old Adam," or "the old self" (Ephesians 4:22); it is also called "flesh" (John 3:6; Romans 7:18), or "original sin," because it refers to the origin of sin among humanity. This is not a sin which we commit but is the evil condition of our nature, which we have by birth. No one is born with some good inside. The Scriptures teach that all people are totally corrupt by nature. "That which is born of the flesh is flesh" (John 3:6). "Behold, I was brought forth in iniquity, and in sin did my mother conceive me" (Psalm 51:5).

By Nature All Are Enemies of God

Because of this evil condition in us we all by nature are inclined to evil, spiritually blind and dead, and enemies of God. "For I know that nothing good dwells in me, that is, in my flesh" (Romans 7:18). "The intention of man's heart is evil from his youth" (Genesis 8:21). "No one understands; no one seeks for God. All have turned aside; together they have become worthless; no one does good, not even one." (Romans 3:11–12). Man by nature does not fear, love, and trust in God. Man, who by his own free will departed from God, cannot by his own reason, strength, and will return to God. "The natural person does not accept the things of the Spirit of God, for they are folly to him, and he is not able to understand them because they are spiritually discerned" (1 Corinthians 2:14). Christians, too, by nature "were dead in trespasses and sin" (Ephesians 2:1).

Disobedience in Action

Original sin causes man to commit all manner of actual sins. "The diseased tree bears bad fruit" (Matthew 7:17). "For out of the heart come evil thoughts, murder, adultery, sexual immorality, theft, false witness, slander" (Matthew 15:19). An "actual sin" is every act against a commandment of God in thought, desire, word, or deed. They are called "actual" sins, not in the sense as though they only were really and truly sin, but because we act, or do, them. These are called sins of commission, because we commit them.

Original sin also leads us to neglect to do what we ought to do. These are called sins of omission, because we omit to do what we should do. The priest and the Levite in the parable of the Good Samaritan (Luke 10:30–37), who passed by the man fallen among the thieves, were guilty of a sin of omission; they failed in their opportunity to help. No one by nature is desirous of doing what God demands; there is not even a willingness to obey God.

The net result of it all is that natural man cannot keep God's commandments in the least part. "They have all turned aside; together they have become corrupt; there is none who does good, not even one" (Psalm 14:3). "Surely there is not a righteous man on earth who does good and never sins" (Ecclesiastes 7:20). "We have all become like one who is unclean, and all our righteous deeds are like a polluted garment" (Isaiah 64:6). The Bible is realistic about our natural condition, as every honest self-examination will show. "If we say we have no sin, we deceive ourselves, and the truth is not in us" (1 John 1:8).

SIN'S EFFECT
ON THE NATURAL KNOWLEDGE OF THE LAW

Through man's fall into sin man's natural knowledge of the Law was indeed obscured but not totally effaced; it was dimmed but not entirely erased. To this day all humanity has by nature some knowledge of God's Law, according to which their conscience judges their thoughts, words, and deeds. Cf. Romans 2:14–15. This inborn knowledge of the Law is furthermore darkened and suppressed in various degrees under the influence of sinful habits and customs. Men "became futile in their thinking, and their foolish hearts were darkened" (Romans 1:21). Cf. Ephesians 4:17–19. Yet there is sufficient knowledge of the Law in all to convict mankind of sinfulness and guilt before God. Cf. Romans 1:32; 3:19–20. This accounts for the presence of religious instincts found in human beings by nature everywhere.

The Tragedy of Sin

Sin is the one great tragedy in life. It makes living after God's design on earth impossible and robs us of dwelling forever with God in the hereafter. In their state of perfection, Adam and Eve would have lived forever. Sin changed that prospect to become death—temporal and eternal death. "The soul who sins shall die" (Ezekiel 18:20). "The wages of sin is death" (Romans 6:23). Sin will not go unrewarded or unpunished. "Sin when it is fully grown brings forth death" (James 1:15). If it were not for Christ's fulfillment of God's Law for us, there would be no escape from the tragic prospect that sin invariably and unalterably offers to us. Sin is the great despoiler.

CHAPTER 6

Knowledge of Sin through the Law

There is but one standard by which man is to judge his life. It alone will reveal how good or how evil he is. This standard is not man-made. The external circumstances in the world or the changing moods and whims of humanity cannot alter it. It comes from God, our Creator, and is set down in the Law, or the Ten Commandments. Neither the laws of any government nor the generally accepted ideas of goodness among men are to determine the righteousness or the sinfulness of man before God. God has set the standard, and His standard never changes. It applies to man throughout the ages. The measure of man's goodness is the Law of God.

THE REVEALED MORAL LAW

The moral law, set down in the Ten Commandments, was given by God Himself to Moses on Mount Sinai (Deuteronomy 4:13), through whom it was published on two tables of stone (Exodus 31:18). The Ten Commandments are recorded in the Bible in Exodus 20 and in Deuteronomy 5:6–22, and are a fuller exposition of the Law as found in the heart of natural man.

The authority of the holy and almighty God stands behind each commandment. "I am the LORD your God" (Exodus 20:2) is joined to the First Commandment and has a bearing on all commandments. No one may invalidate the least of these commandments either for himself or for others.

The moral law is binding on all. "You shall" and "You shall not" are directed to every human being. God insists on strict and perfect obedience. Obedience is not optional, subject to the willingness or the ability of man. It is mandatory. "You therefore must be perfect, as your heavenly Father is perfect" (Matthew 5:48).

God wants the commandments kept out of love to Him. "Love is the fulfilling of the law" (Romans 13:10). Any other motive, like fear of punishment or a desire for glory and reward, is not keeping the Law in the spirit which God demands. God is a "jealous God," which means that He desires and demands complete loyalty and wants all worship and obedience for Himself (Matthew 4:10; Isaiah 42:8) and that He will not tolerate or overlook the slightest departure from His commandments. This applies to our thoughts and desires no less than to our words and acts.

God's Threat and Promise

God says: "I the LORD your God am a jealous God, visiting the iniquity of the fathers on the children to the third and the fourth generation of those who hate Me, but showing steadfast love to thousands of those who love Me and keep My commandments" (Exodus 20:5–6). God will punish man because of his sins, for sin is an insult to the holy and just God. "Cursed be everyone who does not abide by all things written in the Book of the Law, and do them" (Galatians 3:10). The curse includes all manner of punishment and suffering in this life, and eternal death and damnation in the age to come. "The wages of sin is death" (Romans 6:23). Wicked children of wicked parents will be punished for the sins of their parents during their earthly life and, if they persist in their evil ways, will be punished eternally for their own sins; but no one will ever be punished eternally for the sins of others. Even godly children of wicked parents suffer evil results in their earthly life because of their parents' wickedness; this is not a punishment, but rather a trial, which God permits for their eternal good. Sins of the fathers have certain aftereffects, not only in the fathers' lives but also in the lives of their children.

God will graciously reward in body and soul all those who love Him and keep His commandments. This promise is undeserved.

NUMBERING THE COMMANDMENTS

The Lord did not quote the order or the number of the commandments. The commandments divide themselves naturally according to their contents into two groups. The first group contains those which speak of our worship of God and which require a love of God. Cf. Matthew 22:37. The second group contains those which treat of our service to our neighbor and that require a love of man in the same degree as we love ourselves. Cf. Matthew 22:39.

The numbering of the commandments is a human arrangement. The Lutheran Church employs the division of three commandments on the First Table and seven commandments on the Second Table; this numbering is accepted by the majority of Christian people. However, some Christians in their Second Commandment have an elaboration of the First, and so our Second becomes their Third, and in the place of our Ninth and Tenth Commandments they combine these to make the Tenth. The numbering is immaterial, so long as one knows to which particular law of God one is referring.

THE FIRST PURPOSE OF THE MORAL LAW

Before the moral law can serve any other purpose for us—and there are other purposes—it should lead us to a conviction of our sins. That must of necessity be its first purpose, since we are by nature what we are. Like a mirror, the Law shows us our sins. It is a perfectly true reflector, one which never flatters the beholder. The reflection in the mirror of the Law is that of a sinner. "Through the law comes knowledge of sin" (Romans 3:20). "Yet if it had not been for the law, I would not have known sin" (Romans 7:7). Unless we first connect up the Law with an honest examination of self, it can do little good otherwise.

If we do not realize that we are guilty sinners before God, we shall never feel the need of a Savior. Christ, our Savior, has fulfilled the Law for us and paid for the guilt of our transgressions. A review of our life in the light of the Ten Commandments will reveal that we are sinners in need of salvation. "Why then the law? It was added because of transgressions . . . So then, the law was our guardian until Christ came, in order that we might be justified by faith" (Galatians 3:19, 24). The Law keeps alive in us the consciousness of sin and makes us feel the need of a Savior at all times.

The Renewed Heart and the Law

"Christ redeemed us from the curse of the law by becoming a curse for us—for it is written, 'Cursed is everyone who is hanged on a tree'—so that in Christ Jesus the blessing of Abraham might come to the Gentiles, so that we might receive the promised Spirit through faith" (Galatians 3:13–14). Christ has fulfilled the Law for us. This is made known to us in the Gospel, which tells us of our salvation. When the Spirit of God brings us to faith in Christ, He also gives us power and ability to do according to the commandments; He creates in us the love of God and of the brethren. "We love Him because He first loved us" (1 John 4:19). And in view of the fact that by nature we are but dimly conscious of the holy will of God, we are in constant need of the revealed Law as a "rule" to show us the true nature of a God-pleasing life and what are truly good works. The love of God engendered in us by the Spirit of God becomes the motivation of the Christian for obeying the Law.

Our Duty to God, the First Table of the Law

The first three commandments speak of our worship of God and accordingly require of us love of God. They are summed up in these words of Christ: "You shall love the Lord your God with all your heart and with all your soul and with all your mind" (Matthew 22:37).

The First Commandment

"You shalt have no other gods before Me." This is the greatest of all commandments and includes all the rest, for in it God requires the fear and love of God, which is the source from which obedience to all commandments of both tables of the Law must proceed. God wants our very heart, all that we are and have.

Gross Idolatry

"I am the LORD; that is My name; My glory I give to no other, nor My praise to carved idols" (Isaiah 42:8). God prohibits idolatry of every kind. An idol is a false god. We are forbidden to regard and to worship other persons or objects as God. Belief in God without accepting Christ as the Savior is impossible. "All may honor the Son, just as they honor the Father. Whoever does not honor the Son does not honor the Father who sent Him" (John 5:23). Worshiping imaginary beings like Allah of the Muslims or the god of the Unitarians and of Christless lodges is contrary to this commandment. "You shall worship the Lord your God and Him only shall you serve" (Matthew 4:10). Worshiping other persons or objects as God is called gross or coarse idolatry, because it is more easily identified.

Fine Idolatry

There is another kind of idolatry, which is much more common. It is called fine idolatry because it is less easily identified. It is found in the lives of many more people and is no less sinful than is gross idolatry. It consists of responding to others as we should respond only to God. One such example is leaning on our own understanding for spiritual truth instead of accepting in faith the Word of God. "Trust in the LORD with all your heart, and do not lean on your own understanding" (Proverbs 3:5). Another example is letting a fear of men determine our behavior in moral matters rather than doing things out of fear and love to God. "Do not fear those who kill the body but cannot kill the soul. Rather fear Him who can destroy both soul and body in hell" (Matthew 10:28). Another example is loving any sinful way of life and living in it. "For you may be sure of this, that everyone who is sexually immoral or impure, or who is covetous (that is, an idolater), has no inheritance in the kingdom of Christ and God" (Ephesians 5:5). Another example is loving others as we should love God. Jesus says, "Whoever loves father or mother more than Me is not worthy of Me, and whoever loves son or daughter more than Me is not worthy of Me" (Matthew 10:37). Another example is living for material blessings and for this world rather than for God's spiritual blessings and for the world to come. The rich man in the parable lived for material gains and advantages (Luke 16:19), and he was eternally condemned because he worshiped his wealth unto the end. The rich young man loved his possessions more than he loved Christ (Matthew 19:22), which was evident from his refusal to obey Christ; this prompted Christ to speak about the peril of riches.

To Fear, to Love, to Trust in God

The positive side of this commandment is that we fear, love, and trust in God. "To fear God" means to be afraid of the just wrath of God upon disobedience, but especially does it mean to have a respect and an awe for Him, to revere, esteem, and honor Him, and to obey His will. "Let all the earth fear the LORD; let all the inhabitants of the world stand in awe of Him" (Psalm 33:8). "The fear of the LORD is hatred of evil" (Proverbs 8:13). The three men who were thrown into the fiery furnace feared God more than their king (Daniel 3). Daniel feared God more than his king and would rather be thrown into the lions' den than obey a law violating his loyalty to God (Daniel 6). A proper fear of God always goes hand in hand with a love of God and a trust in God. "To love God" means that our highest aim in life should be to be with God and to please Him with loving service; this includes praising God and doing according to His commandments. We should love God with all our heart, with all our soul, and with all our mind (Matthew 22:37). Abraham loved God more than his son Isaac, whom he was asked to sacrifice to God (Genesis 22). "To trust in God" means to believe His Word and to put implicit confidence in His promises; it means that we should not doubt God, nor should we worry and fret but that we depend on Him in every need as we go through life. David trusted in the Lord when he fought Goliath (1 Samuel 17:37, 46–47). "It is better to take refuge in the LORD than to trust in man" (Psalm 118:8). Fear, love, and trust in God go hand in hand and belong together; one cannot do any one without also doing the other. It is God's will that we serve Him with our whole heart and life.

This commandment convicts us all as sinners before God. But thanks be to God, who sent His Son, Jesus Christ, to fulfill this commandment as the sinners' substitute and to bear the guilt and the punishment for the sinners' transgressions of this commandment. "Therefore be imitators of God, as beloved children. And walk in love, as Christ loved us" (Ephesians 5:1–2).

THE SECOND COMMANDMENT

"You shall not misuse the name of the Lord your God." In this commandment God requires of us that we honor His name. Whatever can be said about what God is and what God has done and is doing, properly is God's name. We are not to put these revelations about God to any profane or unworthy use. "In vain" means "without some worthy purpose." "The LORD will not hold him guiltless who takes His name in vain" (Exodus 20:7). As every unprofitable use of God's name is forbidden, so every profitable use of God's name is demanded of us.

The most common abuse of God's name is "cursing by God's name" and "swearing by God's name." These are not identical, though many people erroneously regard them so.

Cursing by God's Name

"To curse" is the opposite of "to bless" and means to wish evil on someone, which is contrary to the Fifth Commandment: "You shall not murder." "To curse *by God's name*" means to call upon God that He should hurt, punish, or damn someone; it also means to speak evil of God and to mock God. "Whoever curses his God shall bear his sin" (Leviticus 24:15). "With it we bless our Lord and Father, and with it we curse people who are made in the likeness of God. From the same mouth come blessing and cursing. My brothers, these things ought not to be so" (James 3:9–10). Peter supported a lie by cursing when he wanted to impress his questioners in the courtyard during the trial of Christ that he had nothing to do with Christ (Matthew 26:74). In our day, cursing is one of the besetting sins in our country.

Swearing by God's Name

"To swear by God's name" means to call upon God to confirm the truth of what we say or promise. This is permissible, even required by God, when it is done to the glory of God and to the welfare of our neighbor. Jesus permitted Himself to be put under oath by the government (Matthew 26:63–64). Abraham for the common good properly put his servant under oath (Genesis 24:3). The apostle Paul swore rightfully (2 Corinthians 1:23). We are, however, not to swear by God's name when we speak lies or when we do it thoughtlessly or when we do it in any sinful, uncertain, or unimportant matters. Peter swore falsely, or to a lie, and thus committed perjury (Matthew 26:72). "You shall not swear by My name falsely" (Leviticus 19:12). King Herod sinned when he swore to do something for the daughter of Herodias, since he did not know what she would ask of him or how important the request would be (Matthew 14:6–9). To swear thoughtlessly and in unimportant matters also is one of the besetting sins in our country.

Superstition

Practice of superstition and efforts to do supernatural things presumably with divine help is contrary to the proper use of God's name. In this category fall fortune-telling, the belief in horoscopes, séances, the supposed power of medicine men and witch doctors in heathen lands, and so on. King Saul sought help of the witch of Endor (1 Samuel 28) and was condemned for it. It would be shocking to know how many dollars are spent on horoscopes and on fortune-telling in our day.

Lying and Deceiving by God's Name

"Lying and deceiving by God's name" means knowingly or unknowingly teaching false doctrine and saying that it is God's teaching. "In vain do they worship Me, teaching as doctrines the commandments of men" (Matthew 15:9). "Behold, I am against the prophets, declares the LORD, who use their tongues and declare, 'declares the LORD' " (Jeremiah 23:31). This manner of vain use of God's name includes covering up an unbelieving heart and a sinful life by a show of piety, which is hypocrisy. Jesus warned against this sin when He said: "Not everyone who says to Me, 'Lord, Lord,' will enter the kingdom of heaven, but the one who does the will of My Father who is in heaven" (Matthew 7:21). According to Jesus, many of the scribes and Pharisees in His day on earth were hypocrites (Matthew 23:13–33). In the early Christian Church Ananias and Sapphira desired to cloak their greed by a gesture of generosity (Acts 5:1–11) and were struck dead by God. There is much of the Pharisee in all of us. Hypocrites often deceive men, hope to but never deceive God, and always deceive themselves. Jesus says of hypocrites: "This people honors Me with their lips, but their heart is far from Me" (Matthew 15:8).

Proper Use of God's Name

In this commandment God lays upon us the duty of using His name reverently, properly, and frequently. Accordingly we are to seek God out by prayer, especially in days of trouble, when we should penitently and trustingly lay our problems before Him. "Call upon Me in the day of trouble; I will deliver you, and you shall glorify Me" (Psalm 50:15). But also at other times should we faithfully pray to God, ask Him for gifts and blessings, such as our daily bread, an understanding heart, success in our work, steadfastness of faith, strength to lead a godly life, and so on. "Ask, and it will be given to you; seek, and you will find; knock, and it will be opened to you" (Matthew 7:7). We should praise God for His greatness and His goodness, for His loving acts in the interest of our spiritual and bodily well-being. We should speak of these things to others. We should show our gratitude to God in prayer to Him and in praise to our fellow men. "Bless the LORD, O my soul, and all that is within me, bless His holy name! Bless the LORD, O my soul, and forget not all His benefits" (Psalm 103:1–2). "Oh give thanks to the LORD, for He is good; for His steadfast love endures forever" (118:1). Jesus commended the one who returned to thank Him for healing him (Luke 17:15–16). The cultivation of thankful remembrance is a very large part of practical Christianity. The use of God's name in praise and thanksgiving is repeatedly requested in many psalms (Psalm 146; 147; 148; 149; 150).

This commandment convicts us all as sinners before God. But thanks be to God, who sent His Son, Jesus Christ, to fulfill this commandment as the sinners' substitute and to bear the guilt and the punishment for the sinners' transgressions of this commandment.

"Therefore be imitators of God, as beloved children. And walk in love, as Christ loved us" (Ephesians 5:1–2).

THE THIRD COMMANDMENT

Meaning of Sabbath

"Remember the Sabbath day by keeping it holy." This law applied only to the Jews under the covenant of the Old Testament. Jesus places it in the same class with the laws concerning sacrifices, as does Paul (Colossians 2:16–17). God gave the Israelites very strict laws regarding the Sabbath. "Sabbath Day" means "rest day." The seventh day of the week was established as a day of rest for the Jews in commemoration of the seventh day of creation week (Exodus 20:8, 11) and of the release of the Jews from the bondage of Egypt (Deuteronomy 5:15). Cessation from work, however, was only a means to an end. The Sabbath Day was a memorial of God's love and kindness, and it was to incite the Israelites to give thanks and praise to God. The Jews kept the Sabbath Day by resting from all regular work and by assembling for religious purposes. In Leviticus 23:3 and Exodus 12:16, we read that the Sabbath was for "a holy convocation," which meant that the Israelites were to assemble for purposes of worship. In Luke 4:16, we read how Jesus, as was His custom, on the Sabbath Day entered the synagogue for the assembly, where He read from the Scriptures.

Although there is no divinely appointed day of rest or of worship in the New Testament, God has told us how to worship Him. Every day is to be for us a day of worship and service dedicated to God. But we are also to meet with our fellow Christians in corporate (group) worship, for the Scriptures state: "Do not neglect to meet together" (cf. Hebrews 10:25). The early Christians assembled in corporate worship (Acts 2:42).

Abolition of Sabbath

Jesus Christ, who as Lord of all has the right over the Sabbath (Matthew 12:8), abolished it and the other Old Testament holy days, which were a shadow of a better rest to come. This spiritual rest came through Christ and His work of redemption. The symbolical meaning of the Old Testament "rest day" lost its significance when Jesus, the true rest for weary sinners, came to redeem sinful mankind by His blameless life and His innocent suffering and death. Therefore the apostle Paul says: "Therefore let no one pass judgment on you in questions of food and drink, or with regard to a festival or a new moon or a Sabbath. These are a shadow of the things to come, but the substance belongs to Christ" (Colossians 2:16–17). When the body came, the shadow lost its significance. It is for this reason that we today are not required to keep the Sabbath day.

Sunday

In fact, God does not command us to observe any particular day. The observance of Sunday does not rest on a command of God. Sunday was chosen by the early Christians as the weekly day of corporate worship probably in commemoration of the resurrection of Christ and because of the outpouring of the Holy Spirit on Pentecost Sunday. Cf. Acts 20:7; 1 Corinthians 16:2. Thus it became customary in the church to meet for public worship on Sunday. The spirit of a special day for group worship lives on in our New Testament Lord's Day. However, every day is to be for Christians a day of worship and service dedicated to the Lord. Cf. Romans 14:5–6; Galatians 4:10–11. We Christians may therefore set aside any day we choose for public worship, and it need not even be one out of seven.

Public Worship

While there is no divine command respecting the observance of any particular day for public worship, it is God's will that we worship Him also in public with our fellow Christians. God has told us how to worship Him. His Word shall be preached. The Sacraments are to be administered. Public prayer and praise shall be in vogue. If this is to be done, it is evident that a certain time and place must be fixed for public worship. The institution or the public ministry or the Word indicates God's will with respect to public worship. Jesus Himself taught the people. He also told His disciples: "The one who hears you hears Me, and the one who rejects you rejects Me, and the one who rejects Me rejects Him who sent Me" (Luke 10:16). He also said: "Blessed rather are those who hear the word of God and keep it" (11:28), and "Whoever is of God hears the words of God" (John 8:47). Of the early Christians we read: "And they devoted themselves to the apostles' teaching and the fellowship, to the breaking of bread and the prayers" (Acts 2:42).

In this commandment God forbids us to neglect the preached or written Word and the Sacraments of Holy Baptism and Holy Communion. A careless use of God's Word is prohibited, when, for example, we do not take to heart what we learn from God's Word, or when we do not live according to it.

Gladly Hear and Learn God's Word

The positive side of this commandment lays on us the duty of holding the Word of God sacred and gladly hearing and learning it. We should treasure what our loving Father in heaven has given us in His Word. Therefore "guard your steps when you go to the house of God. To draw near to listen is better than to offer the sacrifice of fools, for they do not know that they are doing evil" (Ecclesiastes 5:1); "guard your steps" means to watch your step that your heart is not affected by thoughts interfering with true devotion. We should go to church on purpose. Our heavenly Father has important things to tell us. A faithful use of God's Word will bring blessings. By accepting the Gospel we are made wise unto salvation. God's Word warns us against dangers of the soul, trains us in godliness of life, comforts us in trouble, and strengthens us in the hope of life eternal. Mary sat at the feet of Jesus to hear His Word, and Jesus said that she had chosen "the good portion, which will not be taken away from her" (Luke 10:42).

Honor and Support the Ministry

This commandment also includes that we honor and support the preachers and teachers of the Word of God. We should heed the words of God's servants and ambassadors. Thus the apostle Paul told his hearers: "When you received the word of God, which you heard from us, you accepted it not as the word of men but as what it really is, the word of God, which is at work in you believers" (1 Thessalonians 2:13). We are told to be obedient to the Word, with which pastors rule over us, for pastors are ambassadors of God, accountable to Him. "Obey your leaders and submit to them, for they are keeping watch over your souls, as those who will have to give an account. Let them do this with joy and not with groaning, for that would be of no advantage to you" (Hebrews 13:17). We should also contribute to their support and subsistence. "Let the one who is taught the word share all good things with the one who teaches" (Galatians 6:6).

Spread the Word

This commandment includes that we diligently spread the Word of God in all the world. "Go into all the world and proclaim the gospel to the whole creation" (Mark 16:15). This includes personal witness on the part of all of us, and generous moral, personal, and financial support necessary to carry on the program of Christian mission work. Jesus commended the poor widow who gave money for the upkeep of the temple and for the support of the priests (Mark 12:41–44).

In our own personal private life we are to "search the Scriptures because you think that in them you have eternal life; and it is they that bear witness about Me" (John 5:39). Of the Bereans it was said in commendation that they searched the Scriptures daily (Acts 17:11).

Whatever this commandment invites us to do should result in this: "Let the word of Christ dwell in you richly" (Colossians 3:16), that we may believe the right teachings and live according to them.

This commandment convicts us all as sinners before God. But thanks be to God, who sent His Son, Jesus Christ, to fulfill this commandment as the sinners' substitute and to bear the guilt and the punishment for the sinners' transgressions of this commandment. "Therefore be imitators of God, as beloved children. And walk in love, as Christ loved us" (Ephesians 5:1–2).

Our Duty to Our Neighbor, the Second Table of the Law

The last seven commandments treat of our service to our neighbor and, accordingly, require of us a love of man. They are summed up in these words of Christ: "You shall love your neighbor as yourself" (Matthew 22:39).

Our neighbor is everyone who needs our love, and that includes everybody. It is not place but love which makes neighborhood. The parable of the Good Samaritan (Luke 10:25–37) answers the question "Who is my neighbor?" We will miss the chief part of the Second Table of the Law unless we grasp the meaning of who is our neighbor.

We should love our neighbor "as ourselves." We all love ourselves. God wants us to love ourselves and to have a wholesome self-esteem. We are to love our neighbor as sincerely and as constantly as we love ourselves. We are to prove this love by doing as much good to others as we do to ourselves, and as we would have our neighbor do good to us. "So whatever you wish that others would do to you, do also to them, for this is the Law and the Prophets" (Matthew 7:12). However, we should not love ourselves and our neighbor as much as, or more than, we love God. Neither should we love our neighbor for selfish reasons or in anticipation of receiving from him in return for what we do for him. Our love to our neighbor should flow from our fear and love of God.

The Fourth Commandment

"Honor your father and your mother." In this commandment God protects the honor and the office of the authorities, whom He has placed over us as His representatives. The power, control, and sphere of influence which God has given to these authorities depend on their God-appointed stations in life. According to this commandment and other statements of the Scriptures obligations rest upon us as well as upon them.

The First Commandment is basic to all commandments. The Fourth Commandment is a kind of basis for the Second Table of the Law, because a proper understanding of the meaning of authority, personal rights, respect, and obedience will aid us to do what is required in the following commandments. God has also added a promise to this commandment to make it impressive to us. The importance of this promise lies not only in a long life but especially in a good life. This is an undeserved promise, given to make us more willing to keep this and the following commandments.

Our Neighbors in the Home

Our nearest and dearest neighbors are our parents in the home. God has given them first charge over us. They have the greatest responsibility and the largest debt of service to give. Their authority reaches farthest, even into the personal life and affairs of their children. They are to provide for the children and care for them in a material, physical way; but especially are they to feed their souls with the bread of life, for they are to bring up their children "in the discipline and instruction of the Lord" (Ephesians 6:4). The Lord has laid the responsibility for a child's spiritual training primarily upon the parents. Hence they are to set a Christian example in their own life, create a Christian atmosphere in the home, and insist on obedience. In all this the parents are God's representatives. Because they have such a high office and position of influence, they deserve our respect and honor. "Children, obey your parents in the Lord, for this is right. 'Honor your father and mother' (this is the first commandment with a promise), 'that it may go well with you and that you may live long in the land.' Fathers, do not provoke your children to anger, but bring them up in the discipline and instruction of the Lord" (Ephesians 6:1–4). Cf. Colossians 3:20. Our respect and love for our parents should never cease so long as we have them on earth; our age and their age are to be no barrier. The time comes when we must live our own life away from home and when we must assume responsibilities for our own actions; but the time never comes when we may discontinue our love and esteem for our parents. "Let them first learn to show godliness to their own household and to make some return to their parents, for this is pleasing in the sight of God" (1 Timothy 5:4). As in all things, so here Jesus is our example. He was subject to Mary and Joseph (Luke 2:51) and provided for His mother (John 19:26–27).

Our Neighbors in the Church

Next to the home, no earthly place is as exalted as the Christian congregation, where the pastor is the overseer and minister of God in the assembly of believers. In the early days, during the time of our first parents and of the patriarchs, worship services were restricted to the family, with the father as the spiritual overseer. Just when these worship services were enlarged to include numerous families, we do not know. In the church the pastors by virtue of their office are required by God to teach old and young the whole counsel of God, to warn and to correct, to instruct and to comfort. They should do what pleases God and should not cater to the whim and fancy of men. Cf. Titus 1:9. Because of their God-given positions of importance over us, pastors deserve our respect and our prayers. "We ask you, brothers, to respect those who labor among you and are over you in the Lord and admonish you, and to esteem them very highly in love because of their work" (1 Thessalonians 5:12–13). It is of great importance that the dignity of the ministerial office should be guarded and that mere suspicions and conjectures about the pastor's life should not be permitted to hinder the course of the Gospel. Pastors are subject to suspicion and criticism, partly from jealousy, partly from ignorance. The apostle Paul gives a rule in the matter of accusations against pastors in 1 Timothy 5:19. Cf. Deuteronomy 19:15. Pastors hold a high and responsible position. "Obey your leaders and submit to them, for they are keeping watch over your souls, as those who will have to give an account. Let them do this with joy and not with groaning, for that would be of no advantage to you" (Hebrews 13:17).

Our Neighbors in the State

The state, or civil government, also is an authority, which grew out of the home to include larger circles of people as living became more complex and interrelated. The domain of civil governments is the public relation of people to one another, so that all people may live together in peace and security. Civil governments are of God, and rulers are servants of God. They owe it to their subjects to deal righteously and justly, to counteract evil, and to reward the good. They administer the law. We may appeal to the courts of the land to maintain our rights among men. The government exists "to punish those who do evil and to praise those who do good" (1 Peter 2:14). We owe it to God and to our fellow men to be obedient to the laws of the land; and that applies also when no one is looking. We should pay our taxes and perform all the other duties of a patriotic citizen. "Render to Caesar the things that are Caesar's" (Matthew 22:21).

> Let every person be subject to the governing authorities. For there is no authority except from God, and those that exist have been instituted by God. Therefore whoever resists the authorities resists what God has appointed, and those who resist will incur judgment. . . . For he is God's servant for your good. . . . Therefore one must be in subjection, not only to avoid God's wrath but also for the sake of conscience. For because of this you also pay taxes, for the authorities are ministers of God, attending to this very thing. Pay to all what is owed to them: taxes to whom taxes are owed, revenue to whom revenue is owed, respect to whom respect is owed, honor to whom honor is owed. (Romans 13:1, 2, 4, 5–7) Cf. 1 Timothy 2:1–4.

Our Neighbors in the School

Moral education and training in the arts and sciences, which originally flourished chiefly in the family circles, in time were carried out in schools, to which parents sent their children and where teachers were engaged. Today we have public schools and church schools. Church schools stress moral and religious education and teach the arts and sciences in a Christian environment and under the guidance of Christian teachers. Public schools are necessarily limited to the teaching of the arts and sciences. Public school teachers also have the responsibility for teaching social ethics, the standard of good behavior of people toward one another, individually or in groups. Since they are agents of the state, which has no right or duty to teach religion, public schools may not bring religion to bear upon education but must limit themselves to the implications of morality and decency as required by the laws of the state. In all schools the teachers are to be men and women of high moral character, who deal honestly and impartially with the students, and who seek to do their best to train and to instruct them. Few callings are as high as that of a teacher. Teachers should be examples of high morals and good behavior and should be conscientious in their work. Students should give attentive heed to what is taught, should apply themselves diligently, and follow whatever good counsel is given to them; they should respect their teachers.

Our Neighbors in Business and at Work

Industry, the development of business, and the building of factories and offices are the outgrowth of the development of the arts and sciences. As humanity's abilities from God gave rise to inventions and discoveries, trades and professions came into being, manufacturing developed, and the employer-employee relationship was a natural result. Employers have a duty to their workers. They should have an honest regard for the life and well-being of their employees. They should seek to develop a spirit of harmony and cooperation for the good of the employer, the employee, and the general public, whom they serve with their products. Our employers are over us; their authority is limited by the contract of employment. We are to render willing and faithful service as their hired workers. "Bondservants, obey your earthly masters with fear and trembling, with a sincere heart, as you would Christ, not by the way of eye-service, as people-pleasers, but as bondservants of Christ, doing the will of God from the heart, rendering service with a good will as to the Lord and not to man, knowing that whatever good anyone does, this he will receive back from the Lord, whether he is a bondservant or is free. Masters, do the same to them, and stop your threatening, knowing that He who is both their Master and yours is in heaven, and that there is no partiality with Him" (Ephesians 6:5–9). Cf. 1 Peter 2:18.

Whatever our relations may be, we are not to look down on the authorities who are over us, to think little of them, to mock, to ridicule them, or to be ashamed of them. We are not to give them impudent backtalk, to disobey, to resist them, to rebel against them. Our superiors have a right to reprimand and to punish us within the limits of their authority.

We are to honor, serve, and obey our superiors and hold them in love and esteem. We are to be obedient to them, if their request is not contrary to God's Law and if it is within the scope and sphere of their authority. "We must obey God rather than men" (Acts 5:29). A proper regard for this commandment on the part of our superiors and on our part will determine much for a proper regard for the following commandments of the Second Table of the Law.

This commandment convicts us all as sinners before God. But thanks be to God, who sent His Son, Jesus Christ, to fulfill this commandment as the sinners' substitute and to bear the guilt and the punishment for the sinners' transgressions of this commandment. "Therefore be imitators of God, as beloved children. And walk in love, as Christ loved us and gave Himself up for us" (Ephesians 5:1–2).

THE FIFTH COMMANDMENT

"You shall not murder." In this commandment, God protects our and our neighbor's life and well-being. Human life is a sacred thing; it is God's most precious earthly gift to man. "The Spirit of God has made me, and the breath of the Almighty gives me life" (Job 33:4). Cf. Job 10:8–12; Psalm 139:13–16. Because the Lord gives life, He alone has the right to take it. Cf. Acts 17:26; Job 1:21. God may take life when He pleases. "You return man to dust. ...You sweep them away as with a flood. ...Like grass that is renewed in the morning: in the morning it flourishes and is renewed; in the evening it fades and withers" (Psalm 90:3, 5, 6).

Allowable Exceptions

The government has the right to inflict capital punishment on murderers and to wage just wars in defense of the people. The government "does not bear the sword in vain. For he is the servant of God, an avenger who carries out God's wrath on the wrongdoer"

(Romans 13:4). We may defend ourselves if we are attacked; and if in defense of our life we are compelled to hurt and kill, neither the law of the state nor the Law of God will hold us guilty. Cf. Exodus 22:2.

False Notions Exposed

Aside from the exceptions mentioned above, we are not permitted to take life, neither our own nor that of our fellow men. "All who take the sword will perish by the sword" (Matthew 26:52). Explaining every suicide as an irresponsible act of a neurotic or psychotic person is not in conformity with the Scriptures. Mercy killing (euthanasia), the intentional cutting short of human life in the case of disease or illness that may be pronounced incurable and is at the same time very painful, is contrary to this commandment; Christians do not by wrong means seek to escape the sorrows, tribulations, and trials of life. Those who involuntarily shorten their life or impair their health by indulgence in some hurtful habit are transgressors of this commandment. Intemperance in eating, drinking, or even working, is sin.

Murdering with the Tongue

Neither are we permitted to do or say anything which may in some way destroy, shorten, or embitter our neighbor's life, as, for example, the sons of Jacob embittered their father's life (Genesis 42:36–38) or as the prodigal son did to his father (Luke 15:11–32). Some of these mental torments are not considered to be so grievous an offense by many people because they seldom involve a physical action. However, more murdering and suffering are inflicted by hateful words than by leaden bullets. The tongue kills more people than the hand.

Murder Proceeds from Heart

Even when others have wronged us, it is sinful for us to seek revenge. "Beloved, never avenge yourselves, but leave it to the wrath of God, for it is written, 'Vengeance is mine, I will repay, says the Lord' " (Romans 12:19). God forbids us to bear anger and hatred in our hearts against anyone. "But I say to you that everyone who is angry with his brother will be liable to judgment" (Matthew 5:22).

"Everyone who hates his brother is a murderer, and you know that no murderer has eternal life abiding in him" (1 John 3:15). Murder, also murder in act, begins in the heart. "For out of the heart come evil thoughts, murder, adultery, sexual immorality, theft, false witness, slander" (Matthew 15:19). Even the thought of doing evil, or the wish that our neighbor might get hurt or harmed, is a sin. Personal resentment against anyone is sin. We should hate sin, but not the person who sinned against us.

Murder by Means of Inactivity

This commandment also tells us that we are not to omit deeds of love. Failure to help someone makes us as guilty as though we positively harmed someone. The priest and the Levite who passed by the man fallen among the thieves in the parable of the Good Samaritan were guilty because they failed to help this man (Luke 10:30–37). The rich man in the parable of the Rich Man and Lazarus stands condemned by Jesus not because he was wealthy or because of what he did, but because of what he failed to do; he had the ability and the opportunity to help Lazarus, but he had no love in his heart to do so (Luke 16:19–31).

Help and Befriend Everyone

The child of God will, in accord with this commandment, help and befriend his neighbor, give him what he needs for his bodily care during emergencies and dangers, and will act as a true friend when he is forsaken and alone. This should be done not only to our friends but also to our enemies. "To the contrary, 'if your enemy is hungry, feed him; if he is thirsty, give him something to drink; for by so doing you will heap burning coals on his head' " (Romans 12:20). Kindness will melt the enemy into penitence and love. We are to do this not only when "it pays us" to do so but also when there is no promise of a return for our kindness. We should have a sincere compassion and pity with our neighbor in his need. Cf. Matthew 5:7. Jesus is our greatest example. His life on earth was filled with deeds of love.

Qualities of Love

We should also be kind to our neighbor in our words and dealings, be patient, gentle, not easily provoked and angered, even when our neighbors are gruff and insulting. "Blessed are the meek, for they shall inherit the earth" (Matthew 5:5). Those who are gentle and forgiving, patient under injuries, disposed not to render evil for evil, will receive and enjoy every earthly and spiritual blessing that is for their best good here and hereafter. We should always be in a forgiving spirit and should not nurse a grudge. We should pray that evildoers may see the error of their way so that they will accept our forgiveness for Jesus' sake. To be forgiving does not mean to condone evil, to overlook wrong, but it means always to be willing and ready to forgive, and to forget when the evil has been righted. Joseph was sold into slavery by his brothers (Genesis 37:23–35); when they later showed that they were sorry, Joseph forgave them, and he told them that while they meant evil, God turned the evil into good (45:1–16; 50:15–21). Cf. Ephesians 4:32. In Matthew 18:15–18, Christ gives us instructions how we are to proceed against anyone who has wronged us. Summing it all up, we are to strive to do, consistent with Christian principle, what the apostle Paul tells us: "If possible, so far as it depends on you, live peaceably with all" (Romans 12:18).

If we want to find out how precious human life is and see its true value, we will go to Calvary, where God paid the price to redeem each and every soul. The price of redemption was giving His Son into death.

This commandment convicts us all as sinners before God. But thanks be to God, who sent His Son, Jesus Christ, to fulfill this commandment as the sinners' substitute and to bear the guilt and the punishment for the sinners' transgressions of this commandment. "Therefore be imitators of God, as beloved children. And walk in love, as Christ loved us and gave Himself up for us" (Ephesians 5:1–2).

THE SIXTH COMMANDMENT

"You shall not commit adultery." In this commandment God requires of us to discipline our most powerful physical instinct, the sexual instinct. God gave us sex; He designed it; it is wholly good and not to be regarded as something evil. The genuine pleasures of sex are experienced only as it is used according to its Creator's design. Cf. 1 Thessalonians 4:1–5. Promiscuity is normal among animals, but it is not to be so among men. For man God instituted marriage.

Sex Education Advocated

To aid in conforming to this commandment, sex education is advocated. Sex belongs to the moral law. Real sexual attraction is a sacred thing implanted by God Himself. Sex education means the proper instruction by the right teachers under the right conditions. The home is the first teacher, and the father is the right teacher of the boy, and the mother of the girl. It is not well when children learn about sex and its functions from schoolmates or in the streets. In addition to the parents, the church and the medical profession may be helpful in this instruction, which might be given at the time of puberty, when the physical beginning of manhood and womanhood takes place. It is also well to place into the hands of adolescents at a later date a good book on sexuality and its functions in relation to marriage.

Marriage

Marriage is a lifelong union of one man and one woman by mutual consent unto one flesh. It was instituted by God in the Garden of Eden, when God specifically created Eve for Adam (Genesis 2:18–24). Polygamy, plurality of wives, is contrary to God's arrangement. "Each man should have his own wife and each woman her own husband" (1 Corinthians 7:2). In the sight of man, matrimony begins with the wedding ceremony. Marriage is preceded by a rightful betrothal or engagement, which consists in the mutual promise and public declaration to be husband and wife. We have an example in Mary and Joseph (Matthew 1:18–25). Cf. Deuteronomy 22:23–24. Matrimony is a lifelong union; it is dissolved by death of either the husband or the wife (Romans 7:2) and is not continued in heaven (Matthew 22:30). A widow or a widower may marry again (Romans 7:3).

Purposes of Marriage

Marriage has several God-given purposes. (1) Marriage is a relationship of living together for mutual care and assistance. It provides companionship. "Then the LORD God said, 'It is not good that the man should be alone; I will make him a helper fit for him' " (Genesis 2:18). (2) Marriage has been instituted for the propagation of the human race, or the procreation of children. "And God blessed them. And God said to them, 'Be fruitful and multiply and fill the earth' " (Genesis 1:28). Parents beget not only the bodies but living children; therefore also the rational soul is passed on by parents to their children. (3) Marriage was instituted for legitimate sexual intercourse. "But because of the temptation to sexual immorality, each man should have his own wife and each woman her own husband" (1 Corinthians 7:2). Marriage should be entered upon in sanctification, with a full sense of the moral dignity of the relationship. All sinful abuse, all carnal excesses, are to be excluded, according to 1 Thessalonians 4:4–5. Christian husbands and wives will guide themselves according to 1 Peter 3:1–7.

Unclean Thoughts, Desires, Words, and Deeds Are Forbidden

In this commandment God forbids all unclean thoughts, desires, words, and deeds in relation to sex. What may be lawful and pure within wedlock may be a sin and a shame outside of wedlock. Cf. Hebrews 13:4. The philosophy of loose morals and sexual license in our age, both inside and outside of marriage, does not alter God's prohibitions. Acts of fornication, sexual immorality, self-pollution, filthy talking, salacious and dirty jokes, suggestive movements of the body, lustful expressions of the eye, immodest clothes or lack of clothing to arouse sexual desires, cherishing impure thoughts and desires in the heart, are forbidden. "For out of the heart come evil thoughts, murder, adultery, sexual immorality, theft, false witness, slander" (Matthew 15:19). "But I say to you that everyone who looks at a woman with lustful intent has already committed adultery with her in his heart" (Matthew 5:28). One example is Potiphar's wife (Genesis 39:7–12). "But sexual immorality and all impurity or covetousness must not even be named among you, as is proper among saints. Let there be no filthiness nor foolish talk nor crude joking, which are out of place, but instead let there be thanksgiving" (Ephesians 5:3–4). "Abstain from the passions of the flesh, which wage war against your soul" (1 Peter 2:11). In the marital estate God forbids the breaking of the marriage vow. "So they are no longer two but one flesh. What therefore God has joined together, let not man separate" (Matthew 19:6).

Adultery is voluntary sexual relations of a married person with anyone other than the lawful mate. Fornication is a sexual act between unmarried persons; in the Bible this term is used to include also adultery.

Beautiful Within

God requires of us that we lead a clean and decent life in thoughts, desires, words, and deeds. We should strive to be pure and clean in heart, be decent in our behavior, dress, and actions. Our bodies are the temple of God. "Whatever is pure . . . whatever is commendable, if there is any excellence, if there is anything worthy of praise, think about these things" (Philippians 4:8). "Let no corrupting talk come out of your mouths, but only such as is good for building up, as fits the occasion, that it may give grace to those who hear" (Ephesians 4:29).

Married People

Of married people God requires that they love and honor each other, the husband his wife as his God-given helper, and the wife her husband as her God-given head. "Now as the church submits to Christ, so also wives should submit in everything to their husbands. Husbands, love your wives, as Christ loved the church and gave Himself up for her" (Ephesians 5:24–25). Cf. 1 Peter 3:6–7; Colossians 3:19; Ephesians 5:22. The husband is not to be a self-willed master; neither is the wife to be regarded as a slave; both are accountable to God in fulfilling the obligations of their respective positions. Cf. 1 Corinthians 7:3–4.

Regarding Divorce

While voluntarily contracted, marriage may not be voluntarily dissolved. Because God has joined husband and wife together, this union cannot be broken without someone committing a grave sin. Marriage may be dissolved by the innocent party if the mate is guilty of fornication (adultery) or is unfaithful to the marriage vow (1 Corinthians 7:15). In such cases the innocent party has God's permission to secure a legal divorce and is free to marry another person. God, however, does not demand that such action must be taken. A divorce obtained for any other reason may be valid before the law of the land but is not so before God. Something that may be legally right so far as the law of the land is concerned may be morally wrong so far as God is concerned. We cannot say that a divorce is necessarily justified because it has the sanction of the state.

Factors Contributing to Divorce

In the days of the Savior's earthly ministry the laws governing divorce were very lax. Jesus severely rebuked this spirit of laxity; cf. Matthew 19:4–9; Luke 16:14–18. In our day the situation is not any better. Men and women seem to take each other on approval and turn their partner adrift whenever it pleases either one to do so. More and more people are flouting God's laws regarding marriage. Several factors have contributed to this practice. (1) The philosophy of "free love" is being advocated in much of today's reading material, stage plays, and screen presentations at the theaters. This, together with the philosophy of some psychiatrists and marriage counselors, has stamped approval on easy marriage and easy divorce. Uninhibited love-making is the spirit of the age, and it is countenanced on the grounds that the natural sexual instinct should not be unduly repressed. Lack of self-discipline and a disregard for God's Law is the cause of loose morals regarding sexual expression in our day. (2) A second factor is hasty marriages. Failure to learn one's life partner sufficiently before marriage and permitting an emotional love for a partner to be decisive in the choice is a mistake commonly made today. All people have their strength and their weakness, their good points and their bad points, when one considers natural temperament and disposition. Failure to realize this fact will lead to disillusionment in marriage, and the result often is divorce when adjustments are not made. "Before marriage keep both eyes open, and after marriage keep one eye shut," someone has said. We must realize that in marriage we take each other "for better or for worse," and we must be adjustable to that fact. (3) A third factor is the high nervous tension under which we live in our day, wherein we allow ourselves little time for thoughtful reflection. Hasty actions and reactions, hasty decisions and conclusions are the result. Patience is worn thin. Married people must realize that they must work at marriage to be successful.

Weapons of Defense

To overcome all impure sexual thoughts and desires and to keep marriage on an even keel is the effort that every child of God will make. (1) The most potent weapon is the use of God's Word and prayer. Pray to God for a clean heart, and pray for each other, especially for your partner in marriage. (2) Another weapon against immorality and incompatibility is to keep ourselves wholesomely occupied. "The devil tempts every man, but the idle man tempts the devil," so the saying goes. When David was idle, he fell into sin and took Uriah's wife to himself (2 Samuel 11); had he been fighting with his armies, where he belonged, this evil distraction would not have arisen. (3) Temperate eating and drinking also are important, for excessive indulging leads to evil. When the body becomes sluggish, it has an evil effect on the mind and the thought processes. (4) Furthermore, we must not expose ourselves to temptation and therefore should avoid places and situations where we are likely to be tempted to such sins and where impure lusts are aroused. There is much in our day that may lead to the breakdown of the moral fiber and be an occasion of falling prey to sin.

This commandment convicts us all as sinners before God. But thanks be to God, who sent His Son, Jesus Christ, to fulfill this commandment as the sinners' substitute and to bear the guilt and the punishment for the sinners' transgressions of this commandment. "Therefore be imitators of God, as beloved children. And walk in love, as Christ loved us and gave Himself up for us" (Ephesians 5:1–2).

Children of God strive to destroy the root out of which all the branches of sin grow, for they pray to God: "Create in me a clean heart, O God, and renew a right spirit within me."

THE SEVENTH COMMANDMENT

"You shall not steal." In this commandment God protects man's right to own property and material things. Material blessings are given by God as He wills (Jeremiah 27:5). Under God's providence some people become rich, others poor (1 Samuel 2:7). To obey this commandment, we must recognize God as the giver of all material blessings, and we must also realize that we are not the real owners but only the stewards of God, who are managing His goods.

God by law protects our and our neighbor's property because of man's selfishness. Without such protection the industrious and the thrifty would be at the mercy of the lazy and the wicked.

Honorable Ways to Wealth

There are four honorable ways in which man may come into ownership of material possessions: (1) we may buy it or work for it; (2) we may accept it as a donation or by inheritance; (3) we may find it and not be able to restore it to the owner; (4) we may make a fair bid. Every other method of securing possessions is stealing.

God forbids every kind of robbery, theft, and fraud, as well as envious, sinful longings for anything that belongs to our neighbor. Included are cheating, profiteering, charging too much interest, paying unfair wages, being unfaithful in our work, being lazy, and so on. Cf. Ephesians 4:28; Leviticus 19:35–36; Jeremiah 22:13; Psalm 37:21; Proverbs 29:24. While many people do not regard gambling a serious offense and while certain states allow some types of gambling, it is an obvious transgression of this commandment.

Stewards Accountable to God

As stewards of God we must give an account as to how we acquire and how we use our material possessions. We should use them for our own and our neighbor's support. "Do not neglect to do good and to share what you have, for such sacrifices are pleasing to God" (Hebrews 13:16). Cf. 1 Timothy 5:8. We are to use our goods to help those who are in need. "Whoever is generous to the poor lends to the LORD, and He will repay him for his deed" (Proverbs 19:17). We are also to use our possessions and money in the support of the Church. "Let the one who is taught the word share all good things with the one who teaches" (Galatians 6:6)

Ownership is a relative matter. Before man we are the owners and proprietors of what is lawfully ours (Acts 5:4). Communism, which denies the right of private property, finds no support in this commandment or elsewhere.

A Loving Concern for Others

God desires that we help our neighbor to improve and to protect his property and business against loss and damage. We are to take care of his things as well as we do of our own. We are to give him good advice and lend him a helping hand. This act of love encompasses much and may include finding profitable employment for him, improving his work, helping him to be successful in his business and profession, and so forth. We need the indwelling of God's Spirit to do this, for our natural heart is envious and does not want others to succeed beyond us.

Much of our modern business practice is selfish and cruel, where men seek their own advantage and thus squeeze and freeze their neighbor out of his job or his business. The employer-employee relationship would be much helped if all were intent upon doing according to this commandment.

Without Envy

God wants us to rejoice at the prosperity and success of our neighbor and wants us to help him prosper. In helping our neighbor, we should not seek our own honor and profit, but only his good. Christian love "does not insist on its own way" (1 Corinthians 13:5). "So whatever you wish that others would do to you, do also to them, for this is the Law and the Prophets" (Matthew 7:12). God's children seek to love their fellow men as they love themselves.

This commandment convicts us all as sinners before God. But thanks be to God, who sent His Son Jesus Christ to fulfill this commandment as the sinners' substitute and to bear the guilt and the punishment for the sinners' transgressions of this commandment. "Therefore be imitators of God, as beloved children. And walk in love, as Christ loved us and gave Himself up for us" (Ephesians 5:1–2).

THE EIGHTH COMMANDMENT

"You shall not give false testimony against your neighbor." Our good name is a precious gift of God. Next to life it is God's greatest treasure on earth. God here protects us and our neighbor from defamation and slander. We are to respect our neighbor's good name and reputation.

Forbidden Matters

God forbids that we make an untrue statement against our neighbor anywhere, whether that be in court under oath or anywhere in our social contacts. God does not want us to lie about our neighbor or to him; neither are we to withhold the truth in order to harm him. Cf. Proverbs 19:5. To praise men with our mouth when we do not mean it in our heart is deceitful. Neither are we to reveal anything our neighbor has confided to us, or whatever secrets we may otherwise know about him, which, when revealed, are likely to hurt his reputation or do him other harm. "Whoever goes about slandering reveals secrets, but he who is trustworthy in spirit keeps a thing covered" (Proverbs 11:13). Neither are we to speak evil behind our neighbor's back, to spread false reports and hearsay, or even true statements about his faults. We are not to defame him, to "run him down." We dare not rashly condemn our neighbor on gossip. It is also a breach of charity to believe rumors of evil regarding him. When the Bible says, "Judge not, and you will not be judged; condemn not, and you will not be condemned" (Luke 6:37), it is not referring to the judging of erring brethren, which we should do according to God's will; it rather refers to an *officious* judging and condemning either of his person or his manner of life. God also forbids evil thoughts against our neighbor, imagining evil without proof. Suspicion is the false witness of the heart. "Do not devise evil in your hearts against one another" (Zechariah 8:17). Nor may we plan or plot evil against our neighbor in our hearts; such people "conceive trouble and give birth to evil, and their womb prepares deceit" (Job 15:35).

If a neighbor is known to have committed some wrong, Jesus tells us that the first step is to go directly to the offender and endeavor lovingly to convince him of wrongdoing and to lead him to see the error of his way. Cf. Matthew 18:15.

Defend and Shield Your Neighbor

We are to defend our neighbor, taking his part and shielding him against false accusations. But we are not to defend a sin or a wrong that he has actually committed. We should speak well of our neighbor by praising his good qualities and deeds as far as it can be done in keeping with the truth. When true accusations are raised against our neighbor, or real faults are pointed out, we should neither magnify nor extenuate them but explain them as best we can. We should not charge him with wicked motives and purposes but explain in his favor whatever can be so explained. We are to put the best construction on his actions, interpreting in his favor whatever may be so construed. We are to defend those who in their absence are talked about in an evil way. Cf. Proverbs 31:8–9. True Christian love will lead one to overlook and to forgive the sins of others. Cf. 1 Peter 4:8; 1 Corinthians 13:7. Jonathan did according to God's will when he spoke well of David before Saul, who hated David (1 Samuel 19:4).

This commandment is probably broken more easily and more often than any other, because it is not taken seriously. But sins against this commandment are not the harmless little vices we like to think they are. Jesus calls liars the children of the devil. Cf. John 8:44–45. He wants us to love our neighbor.

Of Himself Jesus said: "I am the way, and the truth, and the life. No one comes to the Father except through Me" (John 14:6). If Jesus is truth, then His children should be like Him, truthful. "Let each one of you speak the truth with his neighbor" (Ephesians 4:25). "Do not lie to one another, seeing that you have put off the old self with its practices and have put on the new self, which is being renewed in knowledge after the image of its creator" (Colossians 3:9–10). "Lying lips are an abomination to the LORD, but those who act faithfully are His delight" (Proverbs 12:22).

This commandment convicts us all as sinners before God. But thanks be to God, who sent His Son Jesus Christ to fulfill this commandment as the sinners' substitute and to bear the guilt and the punishment for the sinners' transgressions of this commandment. "Therefore be imitators of God, as beloved children. And walk in love, as Christ loved us and gave Himself up for us" (Ephesians 5:1–2).

THE NINTH AND TENTH COMMANDMENTS

"You shall not covet your neighbor's house." "You shall not covet your neighbor's wife, or his manservant or maidservant, his ox or donkey, or anything that belongs to your neighbor." In these last two commandments God points particularly to the heart and requires that our hearts be holy and free from every evil lust. God here refers not so much to our sinful acts as He does to the evil promptings and desires of the heart, which lead to acts of sin in thoughts, words, and deeds. The sin of covetousness is a sinful craving; it is evil desire or lust. Men generally do not regard such desires as sin, for they think that if such desires are not acted upon in deeds, they never reach the point where guilt may be attached to them. But that is an altogether wrong conclusion. God for Jesus' sake, who has redeemed us from sin, wants us to have only holy desires and love of God and of all that is good.

The Ninth and Tenth Commandments are similar and may readily be considered together. Both forbid coveting. The Ninth Commandment forbids coveting of fixed possessions, of inanimate things; the Tenth Commandment forbids the coveting of living creatures, which may be enticed away by crafty plans.

What Does Coveting Mean?

"To covet" means to lust, to have an inordinate desire and longing for something, especially for something that belongs to another.

It is not necessarily wrong to desire something. It all depends on what it is and why one longs for it. We should desire spiritual gifts of the kingdom of God (1 Corinthians 12:31; Matthew 6:33–34). We may also desire things that are not forbidden to us, like wisdom, knowledge, ability, skill, and so on. There is nothing wrong in the wish to have a better job, a larger salary, preferment in office, an increase in knowledge, a fuller measure of the "good things" of life. Honestly to acquire and to possess treasures of this world, even in abundance, is in itself not wrong. But we are not to covet things that are forbidden to us or that are not intended for us. Covetousness, in the sense of greed and avarice, is wrong; it is a wish to have by hook or by crook; it is a wish to have at the expense of someone else; it is a desire to take or to keep unjustly what belongs to others; it is a feeling of envy at our neighbor's success. It is discontent of the heart, a dissatisfaction with God's economy in our life, a chafing and fretting because God denied certain things that He never intended for us. Covetousness is not a sin peculiar to one class of people; it is common to all people. "For from the least to the greatest of them, everyone is greedy for unjust gain" (Jeremiah 6:13).

Coveting at Root of All Evil Acts

Evil desire is at the root of every transgression of God's Law in thought, word, and deed. Evil lust is behind every act of murder, adultery, theft, hate, envy, jealousy, and disobedience. "For out of the heart come evil thoughts, murder, adultery, sexual immorality, theft, false witness, slander" (Matthew 15:19). "But each person is tempted when he is lured and enticed by his own desire" (James 1:14). Sinful coveting springs from selfishness and is nurtured by the belief that man is in the world principally for the purpose of acquiring, possessing, and enjoying the things of this world. A covetous individual is never rich toward God. Covetousness is contrary to the spirit of Christ and to the love we should have for our neighbor. It warps personality, destroys brotherly sympathy, kills generosity, stifles good impulses, and frustrates happiness. Therefore "be on your guard against all covetousness" (Luke 12:15). He who covets will often seek to get what he covets, even if he has to employ crafty means to gain his end. This sin is especially aggravated when one secures what one covets "by a show of right," which means giving the false impression that it was rightfully secured.

We Should Have Holy Desires

As the redeemed of the Lord we are to have holy desires. "You shall be holy, for I the LORD your God am holy" (Leviticus 19:2). Cf. Matthew 5:48. "Delight yourself in the Lord, and He will give you the desires of your heart" (Psalm 37:4). Children of God will take delight in God's will and God's ways, pray to Him, and will be satisfied with what God gives them. "But if we have food and clothing, with these we will be content. But those who desire to be rich fall into temptation, into a snare, into many senseless and harmful desires that plunge people into ruin and destruction. For the love of money is a root of all kinds of evils. It is through this craving that some have wandered away from the faith and pierced themselves with many pangs" (1 Timothy 6:8–10). Christians will "through love serve one another" (Galatians 5:13). The apostle Paul showed his love and interest in his fellow men when he returned the runaway servant Onesimus to his master Philemon, as the Epistle to Philemon indicates. Because of Christ's great love to us we will help our neighbor and be of service to him in keeping what he has, will rejoice in his prosperity, will look after his interests, will take care of his things as though they were our own, and will urge his family and friends to remain loyal to him.

Like all commandments, so these last two commandments convict us all as sinners before God. But thanks be to God, who sent His Son, Jesus Christ, to fulfill these commandments as the sinners' substitute and to bear the guilt and the punishment for the sinners' transgressions of these commandments. "Therefore be imitators of God, as beloved children. And walk in love, as Christ loved us and gave Himself up for us" (Ephesians 5:1–2).

How Do We Look
in the Mirror of the Law?

The consideration of the Ten Commandments shows us that we have a large order for our life. An honest self-examination will reveal this result: we have failed to measure up to the Law's demands. Even the most God-fearing person must confess that he falls short in his love of God and in his love of his fellow men. With the apostle Paul we all must say: "For I do not do the good I want, but the evil I do not want is what I keep on doing" (Romans 7:19). This is hard for our old Adam to admit, but it is the truth; it cannot be denied. Truly, "through the law comes knowledge of sin" (Romans 3:20).

CHAPTER 7

Salvation Comes from God

Everywhere man by nature is seeking to get right with what he considers God, and he endeavors to do this by his own efforts. There is one refrain through all man-made (heathen) religions—salvation by works. Self-righteousness is man's prevailing exercise of religion. For most people, even for many within the pale of the Christian Church, the doing of "good deeds" or following the Golden Rule is the way of being saved.

The Law of God is good in itself and shows a perfect way to heaven. "So the law is holy, and the commandment is holy and righteous and good" (Romans 7:12), and "the person who does the commandments shall live by them" (Romans 10:5). To the rich young ruler, who came to Jesus with the question: "What good deed must I do to have eternal life?" Jesus gave this answer: "If you would enter life, keep the commandments" (Matthew 19:17). Cf. Luke 10:26–28. The Law indeed shows a perfect way to heaven, but it is a way which mankind cannot use. The Law promises salvation to man on terms which man cannot fulfill.

It is not the fault of the Law that we cannot save ourselves by it. It is our own fault that we are unable to measure up to its demands. Man's sinfulness makes salvation by the Law impossible. The best we can do is unacceptable to God in every respect. Because of man's sinfulness the Bible says: "No one is justified [declared just and holy] before God by the law" (Galatians 3:11). If the Law is to serve as a way to heaven, it must be perfectly kept. "For all who rely on works of the law are under a curse; for it is written, "Cursed be everyone who does not abide by all things written in the Book of the Law, and do them" (Galatians 3:10).

CHRIST SAVED US BY KEEPING THE LAW

Our salvation must come from a source outside of us, a source that can meet the Law's requirements and pay for man's transgressions of the Law to the satisfaction of God. We have that salvation in Christ Jesus. "And there is salvation in no one else, for there is no other name under heaven given among men by which we must be saved" (Acts 4:12). Jesus Himself says: "I am the way, and the truth, and the life. No one comes to the Father except through Me" (John 14:6). Christ met the Law's demands for us and paid in our place for our transgressions.

WHAT MOVED GOD TO SAVE US?

God's act of salvation was motivated by His undeserved love for mankind. "For God so loved the world, that He gave His only Son, that whoever believes in Him should not perish but have eternal life" (John 3:16). "He saved us, not because of works done by us in righteousness, but according to His own mercy" (Titus 3:5). "By grace you have been saved" (Ephesians 2:8). The grace of God is God's merciful, affectionate disposition and good will to man, according to which He forgives sins to those who are worthy of eternal death. The hymnist Augustus Toplady wrote, "The grace of God always finds us beggars and leaves us debtors."

SALVATION IS AN ACCOMPLISHED FACT

The fact of God's undeserved love is assured us in the Gospels according to Matthew, Mark, Luke, and John, where the life of Christ is portrayed and its purpose made known. In the epistles of Paul, Peter, and John it is reiterated and especially applied to the life of man.

The Bible teaches that God has done everything for man's salvation (Hebrews 7:26–27) and that man cannot and need not add one thing toward his salvation. Salvation is in its entirety a gift of God to be accepted by faith. "For by grace you have been saved through faith. And this is not your own doing; it is the gift of God, not a result of works, so that no one may boast" (Ephesians 2:8–9). This wonderful truth is plainly stated many times in the Scriptures. Salvation is an accomplished fact. It is true and certain, "deserving of full acceptance" (1 Timothy 1:15).

SALVATION IS AVAILABLE FOR ALL MANKIND

Christ's work of redemption is not only for certain peoples and individuals but is for all mankind. "God so loved *the world*, that He gave His only Son" (John 3:16). "God desires *all people* to be saved and to come to the knowledge of the truth" (1 Timothy 2:4).

Christ is "the propitiation [the atonement] for our sins, and not for ours only but also for the sins of *the whole world*" (1 John 2:2). The redemption was also for those who are finally lost because of their own unbelief, as we see from 2 Peter 2:1.

GOD MEANS WHAT HE SAYS

God is always serious and sincere about the salvation of mankind. He does not trifle with the destiny of anyone. "As I live, declares the Lord God, I have no pleasure in the death of the wicked, but that the wicked turn from his way and live" (Ezekiel 33:11). When Jesus beheld the city of Jerusalem and considered the people's guilt and the miseries that were to come on them, He wept over it (Luke 19:41). He said: "O Jerusalem, Jerusalem, the city that kills the prophets and stones those who are sent to it! How often would I have gathered your children together as a hen gathers her brood under her wings, and you were not willing!" (Matthew 23:37).

ALWAYS ABLE TO SAVE

The grace of God in Christ is always able to save; it always is efficacious; it always has the power to impress and to move the heart and to work acceptance of the offer of grace. Its ability to lead men to God is constant. Until the end of time we are living in "favorable time . . . the day of salvation" (2 Corinthians 6:2).

Why Are Not All People Saved?

The reason why some people are not saved is not that Christ is not able and willing to save them or that Christ has not provided a complete salvation for all, but that they refuse the offer of grace. The fault lies in the perverse will of man. Cf. Matthew 23:37; Acts 7:51. If men perish, they will be their own destroyers, and the guilt will forever rest on them.

Salvation Only through Christ

"God was in Christ, reconciling the world to Himself" (2 Corinthians 5:19). Christ reconciled the world to God by offering Himself as propitiation to God for the sins of mankind. He "gave Himself a ransom for all" (1 Timothy 2:6). "He is the propitiation for our sins, and not for ours only but also for the sins of the whole world" (1 John 2:2).

God laid upon Christ, and Christ willingly accepted, the obligation in man's stead both to keep the Law and to bear the punishment the Law exacts of the transgressors. Christ fulfilled the Law in the stead of man. Cf. Galatians 4:4–5. Christ vicariously suffered the punishment that men had incurred by their transgression of the Law. Cf. Galatians 3:13; 2 Corinthians 5:14; 1 Peter 3:18.

Christ in the place of man rendered to God, who was wrathful over the sins of man, a satisfaction that changed His wrath into grace toward men. Therefore we have salvation only through Christ.

Christ Is a Unique Personality

To achieve our salvation for us, Christ had to possess two natures. These two natures are the divine and the human. Christ had the divine nature from all eternity with the Father and the Holy Spirit; He is the everlasting God. Christ assumed the human nature when He was conceived in, and born of, the Virgin Mary. His human nature, therefore, had a beginning. So we confess that Jesus Christ is true God, begotten of the Father from eternity, and also true man, born of the Virgin Mary.

Regarding Christ's *divine nature* the Bible states that the prophets of the Old Testament referred to the coming Savior as one who is true God. Cf. Isaiah 9:6. Christ said of Himself: "I and the Father are one" (John 10:30). The Scriptures ascribe to Jesus divine names (1 John 5:20; John 20:28; Matthew 17:5; Romans 9:5), divine characteristics, or qualities (John 1:1–2; Hebrews 13:8; Matthew 28:20; John 21:17; Matthew 28:18), divine works (John 1:3; Hebrews 1:3; Matthew 9:6; John 5:27), and divine honor and glory (John 5:23; Hebrews 1:6; Revelation 5:12–13).

Regarding Christ's *human nature* the Bible expressly calls Jesus man (1 Timothy 2:5), ascribes to Him a human body and soul (Luke 24:39; Matthew 26:38), ascribes to Him human feelings and actions (Mark 4:38; Matthew 4:2; John 19:28; John 11:35; Matthew 26, 27). While on the basis of Scripture we insist that Jesus assumed a real and true human nature, we must call attention to certain peculiarities of this nature. Jesus was not begotten man in the natural way. Jesus was begotten without a human father, and was born of a virgin, the Virgin Mary, by the Holy Spirit. Cf. Isaiah 7:14; Matthew 1:18, 23; Luke 1:35. Furthermore, Christ was without sin. Cf. John 8:46; 2 Corinthians 5:21; 1 Peter 2:22; Hebrews 7:26. Jesus was personally sinless and therefore not subject to death. When He died on the cross for our sins, He died because He wanted to die and at the very moment He wanted to die. The divine and human natures are united in Christ, both natures together forming one undivided and indivisible person. There are not two Christs but only one Christ. Jesus Christ, who had the divine nature from all eternity, took the human nature into His divine being when He was conceived of the Holy Spirit in the Virgin Mary. This incorporation of the two natures in Christ we call *the personal union* of the two natures, because Christ still is and continues to be one person, one being. The personal union is a profound mystery. Cf. John 1:14; 1 Timothy 3:16; Colossians 2:9.

THE SAVIOR HAD TO BE A TRUE MAN

In order to save man, it was necessary for Christ to do and to suffer what man should have done and suffered; hence He had to become man, that as man's substitute He might act in man's place. "But when the fullness of time had come, God sent forth His Son, born of woman, born under the law, to redeem those who were under the law, so that we might receive adoption as sons" (Galatians 4:4–5). "Since therefore the children share in flesh and blood, He Himself likewise partook of the same things, that through death He might destroy the one who has the power of death, that is, the devil. . . . For surely it is not angels that He helps, but He helps the offspring of Abraham" (Hebrews 2:14, 16).

THE SAVIOR HAD TO BE TRUE GOD

More is required to be mankind's savior than being a human being. A sinful man can fulfill the Law not even for himself, much less for another. Even a saint, if there were such, could keep the Law only for himself, but his obedience could not be credited to anyone else. Cf. Ezekiel 18:20. The redemption of a soul costs so much, requires so much, that man must forever cease in his attempts to redeem himself or his brother. "Truly no man can ransom another, or give to God the price of his life, for the ransom of their life is costly and can never suffice" (Psalm 49:7–8). God alone is not under the Law; so He alone is in position to do something about our salvation. "For as by the one man's disobedience the many were made sinners, so by the one man's obedience the many will be made righteous" (Romans 5:19). Only God could reconcile the world to Himself. The saving value and power of Christ's suffering and death lie in the fact that Jesus was and is God, who according to the human nature suffered and died for us. To be our Savior, Christ had to be God. He had to attach the full weight of His deity to His obedience, suffering, and death, as Scripture tells us in Galatians 4:4–5 and Romans 5:10. Facing death, He had to be the mighty God that He might be able by His death to overcome death, to raise up again the temple of His body (John 2:19, 21), and to take up His life again (John 10:18). Jesus Christ died not simply as any other man, but in and with His death conquered sin, death, hell, and eternal damnation. Scripture bases the redemptive value of the suffering and death of Christ on the very fact that not a mere man but that the Son of God suffered and died (Romans 5:10; 8:32; 1 John 1:7). Only because of His deity could Jesus provide a satisfaction for us.

CHRIST HUMBLED HIMSELF

In order to take man's place under the Law and to fulfill all righteousness for him, and in order to suffer the guilt and the punishment that man deserved because of his sins, Christ had to humble Himself under the Law. "For you know the grace of our Lord Jesus Christ, that though He was rich, yet for your sake He became poor, so that you by His poverty might become rich" (2 Corinthians 8:9).

In Christ, God and man are united in one person. The human nature of Christ, created by God in the Virgin Mary, was taken through the miraculous act of God into the person of the Son of God. This is the incarnation. The resulting wondrous and singular union of God and man into one person (Christ) is called the personal union. Because of the union of God and man in Christ, a communion of natures (the divine and the human) took place. Also a communion of attributes resulted. What the divine and human natures in Christ essentially are, and everything that these natures do or suffer according to their respective essences, are in communion in the person of Christ. Thus Christ's human nature, by virtue of its union with the divine nature, received divine glory. Christ's human nature is invested with divine qualities, such as omnipotence, omniscience, and all the other attributes of the deity. The human nature shares in the divine power and in the other divine properties.

In the light of all this, what do we understand by the humiliation of Christ? The humiliation of Christ consists in this, that Christ refrained, during His earthly life, from the full use of the divine glory which was given to the human nature by virtue of its union with the divine nature. During His life on earth Christ did not fully use His communicated divine attributes. The entire fullness of the divinity, which dwelt in Christ bodily, was concealed and withheld for the greater part at the time of His humiliation. From the time of His conception, even in Mary's womb, Christ had in His possession, also according to His human nature, the divine majesty. However, He laid it aside, and, as Dr. Luther explains, He kept it concealed in the state of humiliation and did not use it always but only when He wished. Another defines the humiliation thus: "The humiliation of Christ pertains to His human nature and consists in this, that Christ for a time abdicated the full use of the divine majesty which the human nature received in personal union with the divine nature by communication" (John William Baier, *Compendium of Positive Theology*). The humiliation was not feigned but a real renunciation of the full and constant use of the divine majesty imparted to Christ's human nature. We cannot with our minds grasp the mystery involved in Christ's state of humiliation. Our reason cannot perceive how this is possible, but we believe it on the basis of Scripture.

For what reason did Christ not fully use the divine attributes according to His human nature during His humiliation? His office as Redeemer required of Him that, in order to carry out the divine plan of redemption, He should in our place be put under the Law and in our stead suffer and die (Galatians 3:13; 4:4–5). To achieve this redemptive work, Christ had to refrain from fully using His divine attributes, qualities, and properties. This nonuse made the genuine human development of Christ possible and made it possible for Him to be our substitute under the Law. Only when the performance of His redemptive work required it (e.g., performing miracles to prove His divinity), did Christ use some of these divine attributes according to His human nature during His earthly life.

The Scriptures describe the humiliation in Philippians 2:5–8, where we read:

> Have this mind among yourselves, which is yours in Christ Jesus, who, though He was in the form of God [Christ was and is of the same essence as God], did not count equality with God a thing to be grasped [He did not make use of His glory and majesty as a prize or spoil, as a victor might display it; He did not make a show of His divinity merely for the sake of gaining favor and making impressions], but emptied Himself [He refrained from using His almighty power and majesty], by taking the form of a servant [became lowly

by not always and fully using His divine qualities; He waived the right and renounced the use of these qualities, without giving up His divine majesty; He took the role of one who ministered unto others], being born in the likeness of men [He did not only become man, but lived under the conditions and after the manner of men, as though He had no divine powers]. And being found in human form [His manner of living was like that of any man], He humbled Himself by becoming obedient to the point of death, even death on a cross.

Christ's humiliation included all His years in the flesh among men, from His conception in the Virgin Mary to His death on the cross, which was the climax of His humiliation.

CHRIST'S MOTIVE IN HUMBLING HIMSELF

Christ's love for sinful mankind prompted Him to humble Himself that He might redeem man from sin, death, and hell. Redemption was altogether in our interest, and it was motivated by Christ's love, which none of us deserved. "By this we know love, that He laid down His life for us" (1 John 3:16). "The Son of God, who loved me and gave Himself for me" (Galatians 2:20). "Walk in love, as Christ loved us and gave Himself up for us, a fragrant offering and sacrifice to God" (Ephesians 5:2).

Christ's humiliation is thus described and confessed in the Apostles' Creed: "Conceived by the Holy Spirit; born of the Virgin Mary; suffered under Pontius Pilate; was crucified, died, and buried." These are sometimes called the stages of Christ's humiliation.

THE CONCEPTION OF CHRIST

Christ was miraculously conceived in the Virgin Mary through the operation of the Holy Spirit. The Scriptures teach that by "the power of the Most High" (Luke 1:35) Christ, the Son of God, received His human body and soul in the Virgin Mary. Christ's conception and birth belong to His humiliation inasmuch as they constitute a lowly mode of becoming man. Jesus was in every respect like other human children, except that He was not begotten of an earthly father and that He was holy. Joseph was Christ's earthly father. Although His mother, Mary, was a sinful woman born of sinful parents, Jesus Himself was without original, or inherited, sin. The very fact that the Son of God assumed the human nature from Mary *by the Holy Spirit* accounts for the sinlessness of the human nature of Christ. So it was the work of the Holy Spirit to produce from the sinful nature of the Virgin Mary the holy nature of Christ. Christ's, and Christ's only, was an immaculate conception. When the angel informed Mary that she was chosen to be the mother of Christ, he said: "The Holy Spirit will come upon you, and the power of the Most High will over-shadow you; therefore the child to be born will be called holy—the Son of God" (Luke 1:35). And to Joseph, who was engaged to Mary, the angel said: "Joseph, son of David, do not fear to take Mary as your wife, for that which is conceived in her is from the Holy Spirit" (Matthew 1:20).

The Birth of Christ

The Scriptures teach that Christ was born of the Virgin Mary a true human child. The nativity of Christ is recorded in Luke 2:1–20 and in Matthew 1:18–25.

The Suffering and Death of Christ

Throughout His earthly life Christ endured poverty, contempt, and persecution. The entire life of Christ during the state of His humiliation was filled with suffering. He bore the weaknesses and infirmities common to man, though He was without sin. Cf. Hebrews 2:17; 4:15. His suffering was intensified in Gethsemane and on Golgotha and reached its climax when He exclaimed on the cross: "My God, my God, why have You forsaken Me?" (Mark 15:34); this describes His suffering of the torments of hell and damnation.

Christ died on the accursed tree of the cross, to which He was condemned by Pontius Pilate after a despicable treatment of mock-ery, ridicule, torture, and physical abuse. The death of Christ was a voluntary act on His part (John 10:15, 17). His death was real; His soul departed from His body. The Bible narrative of Christ's suffering and death is recorded in Matthew 26:36–27:50; Mark 14:32–15:37; Luke 22:39–23:46; John 18:1–19:30.

THE BURIAL OF CHRIST

Christ's body was laid in the grave of Joseph of Arimathea, who had claimed the body from Pilate. Christ's body remained in the grave to the third day but without seeing decay. The soul of Christ was in Paradise (Luke 23:43). The Bible narrative of Christ's burial is recorded in Matthew 27:57–61; Mark 15:42–47; Luke 23:50–56; John 19:38–42.

CHRIST IS EXALTED

Like the humiliation, so the exaltation affects only the human nature of Christ. If the state of humiliation consists in Christ's partial nonuse of the divine majesty by the human nature, His state of exaltation consists in the full use of the divine majesty. The difference between Christ's state of humiliation and His state of exaltation is this, that the use of the divine majesty during the state of humiliation was limited, subject to the demands of Christ's office as the Redeemer of the world, while in the state of exaltation the full exercise, operation, or manifestation of the divine majesty set in. As the soul is operative throughout the body and as fire shows itself in a glowing iron, so Christ in His state of exaltation fully, powerfully, and publicly exercises the divine majesty also according to His human nature. (This was concealed or withheld for the greater part at the time of His humiliation.) Christ has entered His glory, so that now, not only as God but also as man, He knows all things, can do all things, is present with all creatures, and has under His feet and in His hands everything that is in heaven and on earth and under the earth, as He Himself testifies in the Scriptures (Matthew 28:18; John 13:3; Ephesians 4:10). Another explains Christ's state of exaltation thus: "The state of exaltation is that in which Christ, according to His human nature, after laying aside the infirmities of the flesh, assumed and exercised the full use of the divine majesty" (John William Baier, *Compendium of Positive Theology*).

The Scriptures describe the exaltation of Christ in Philippians 2:9–11, where we read:

> Therefore God has highly exalted Him and bestowed on Him the name that is above every name [Christ's name is above all, for He is King over all], so that at the name of Jesus every knee should bow, in heaven and on earth and under the earth [the name of Christ Jesus, which during His humiliation was despised and rejected, is now supreme, that angels and believers willingly and gladly acknowledge and admit that Jesus is Lord; also the unbelievers and the devils will sometime have to acknowledge it, whether they want to or not], and every tongue confess that Jesus Christ is Lord, to the glory of God the Father. [In the end, at the Day of Judgment, every tongue must and will confess that Jesus Christ is Lord; some will do so in adoration, while others will do so in shame and terror.]

By His exaltation Christ brought into full use according to His human nature that divine majesty which is rightfully and properly His because of the personal union of His two natures. It is against the essential character of Christ, the God-man, to be forever humbled according to His human nature.

Christ's state of exaltation is thus described and confessed in the Apostles' Creed: "He descended into hell. The third day He rose again from the dead. He ascended into heaven and sits on the right hand of God the Father Almighty. From thence He will come to judge the living and the dead." These are sometimes called the stages of Christ's exaltation.

THE DESCENT OF CHRIST INTO HELL

The Scriptures teach that Christ, after He was made alive in the grave (the soul had returned to the body), descended into hell, not to suffer, but to proclaim His victory over His enemies. In 1 Peter 3:18–19 we read that Christ was "put to death in the flesh [in the days of His flesh on earth] but made alive in the Spirit [which denotes the new life that began with His becoming alive again], in which He went and proclaimed to the spirits in prison." We do not know the locality of this prison, but it is the place where the souls, or spirits, of those who during their life on earth had been disobedient, are awaiting Judgment Day. Christ did not preach repentance and forgiveness to them, which is impossible according to Hebrews 9:27; but He did preach by manifesting Himself, whom they had rejected, as the victor over death and hell. In what manner this took place, we do not know. The descent into hell probably took place on Easter morning. The Bible does not give us any particulars about the manner of the descent.

THE RESURRECTION OF CHRIST FROM THE DEAD

The Scriptures teach that on the third day after His death Christ victoriously arose from the dead and showed Himself alive to His disciples. The narrative of Christ's resurrection is found in the Bible in all four Gospels (Matthew 28; Mark 16; Luke 24; John 20 and 21). Christ's resurrected body is a spiritual body, which is no longer subject to the laws and conditions to which it was subject before; it does not require food, rest, or such.

THE IMPORTANCE OF CHRIST'S RESURRECTION

Christ's resurrection definitely proves that Christ is what He said He was, namely, the Son of God. Christ was "declared to be the Son of God in power according to the Spirit of holiness by His resurrection from the dead" (Romans 1:4). Jesus Himself pointed to His resurrection as the final proof of His divine mission. Cf. Matthew 12:38–40. The resurrection of Christ proves that the religion He taught is divinely true. Cf. John 7:16; John 8:28.

Christ's resurrection definitely proves that God the Father accepted the sacrifice of His Son for the reconciliation of the world. The apostle Paul says: "If Christ has not been raised, your faith is futile and you are still in your sins" (1 Corinthians 15:17). In Romans 4:25, we read: "Christ was delivered up for our trespasses and raised for our justification." This means that Christ was delivered into death for our sins and that His resurrection proves to us that His suffering and death really did atone for our sins and that we are truly justified before God because of Christ's work of redemption. The resurrection of Christ is the declaration before all the world that the object of His death had been gained, namely, our salvation.

Christ's resurrection definitely proves that there is a resurrection of the dead (1 Corinthians 15:12, 16, 20) and that for the believers in Christ there is a resurrection unto eternal life. Christ says: "Because I live, you also will live" (John 14:19). Again He said: "I am the resurrection and the life. Whoever believes in Me, though he die, yet shall he live, and everyone who lives and believes in Me shall never die" (John 11:25–26).

THE RESURRECTED CHRIST
SEEN BY HIS DISCIPLES

During the forty days following His resurrection Christ did not live with His disciples as He had done for about three years before His suffering and death. But He did repeatedly appear to them at different times and in different places to convince them of the fact of His resurrection, to expound to them the Scriptures (Luke 24:25, 44–45), and to give them further instructions concerning the kingdom of God and their particular mission as His disciples on earth (Acts 1:3–8). "God raised Him on the third day and made Him to appear, not to all the people but to us who had been chosen by God as witnesses, who ate and drank with Him after He rose from the dead" (Acts 10:40–41). Cf. 1 Corinthians 15:4–8.

THE ASCENSION OF CHRIST INTO HEAVEN

The Scriptures teach that Christ, in His human nature, visibly ascended from Mount Olivet into heaven forty days after His resurrection, and entered into the glory of His Father as our forerunner. Cf. Luke 24:50–51; Acts 1:9–11. Heaven is the Father's house in which there are many mansions, where Christ has by His redemptive work prepared a place for us and where we shall be with Him. Cf. John 14:2–3; Philippians 1:23; Hebrews 6:20. While Christ did withdraw His visible presence from this earth, He is really and truly, though invisibly, present with us at all times. He says: "Behold, I am with you always, to the end of the age" (Matthew 28:20).

THE SESSION OF CHRIST
AT THE RIGHT HAND OF GOD

The Scriptures teach that Christ, also according to His human nature, rules and fills all things with divine power and majesty. "Sitting at the right hand of God" is a figure of speech, which means to occupy a position of divine honor "far above all rule and authority and power and dominion, and above every name that is named, not only in this age but also in the one to come" (Ephesians 1:21–22). God "has put all things under His [Christ's] feet." Christ is the supreme Lord, to whom all creatures must yield obedience.

It is of great comfort for us to know that Christ according to His human nature is at the right hand of God. As our exalted Prophet He is sending men to preach the Gospel of redemption. Cf. Ephesians 4:10–12. As our exalted Priest and Advocate He pleads for us before God. Cf. 1 John 2:1; Romans 8:34. As our exalted King He governs and protects His Church, and as head of the Church He rules the world in the interest of His Church. Cf. Matthew 22:44; Psalm 110:1. No matter what may happen, all things work together for the Christians' good. Cf. Romans 8:28–30. We may not always in this life be able to tell how certain things can be advantageous to Christ's Church, but eternity will reveal the wise providence of God.

THE COMING OF CHRIST TO JUDGMENT

The Scriptures teach that Christ will return visibly and in glory. The fact of Christ's return is foretold (Acts 1:11). Cf. Revelation 1:7. He will not come in lowliness, as He did at Bethlehem, but in power and in great glory. Cf. Matthew 25:31. At His coming the resurrection of the dead will take place. Cf. Acts 10:42; 1 Thessalonians 4:15, 16; Revelation 20:13. This present world will be destroyed to make way for a new heaven and a new earth. Cf. 2 Peter 3:10. The purpose of Christ's second coming is to judge the world in righteousness by His

Word. Christ will judge in such a way that everyone will receive full justice. Judgment Day has been appointed by God but is unknown to man. It will come suddenly and unexpectedly, "like a thief" (2 Peter 3:10), and as "the lightning comes from the east and shines as far as the west, so will be the coming of the Son of Man" (Matthew 24:27).

THE THREEFOLD OFFICE OF CHRIST

The purpose of Christ's work of redemption is to save us for time and for eternity to be and to live as God's children. Briefly stated, the work of Christ consists in this: "For the Son of Man came to save the lost" (Matthew 18:11); "Christ Jesus came into the world to save sinners" (1 Timothy 1:15). Whatever Christ did, and still does, serves this one purpose and is motivated by the tender mercies and love of God to man. Thus the work of Christ is a unit, having for its single purpose the salvation of man.

As the name Christ (Anointed) designates, the work of Christ, the Savior, has three distinct phases, all of which were and are concurrently active in His salvation work. On the basis of statements from the Scriptures we speak of Christ as our Prophet, as our Priest, and as our King.

CHRIST AS OUR PROPHET

A prophet is one who speaks for another. A prophet of God is one who speaks for God, making known and interpreting the Word and the will of God to man; he is God's spokesman, representative, ambassador. In the Old Testament days the office of prophet existed among Israel: Moses, Isaiah, Jeremiah, Daniel, and others were prophets.

Christ is a prophet. Concerning Him it was foretold that "the Lord your God will raise up for you a prophet" (Deuteronomy 18:15). In Luke 13:33, Christ refers to Himself as a prophet, and He was regarded by His followers as "a prophet mighty in deed and word before God and all the people" (Luke 24:19). Christ is *the* prophet who revealed Himself by word and deed as the Son of God and the Redeemer of the world. He spoke of Himself and for Himself.

Christ performed His prophetic office not only personally in the days of His flesh among men, but He still performs this office through the ministry of the Word today. Christ charged His disciples to teach all nations the things He had commanded them. Cf. Matthew 28:19–20. "The one who hears you hears Me," said Jesus (Luke 10:16). Cf. Ephesians 4:11–12. Whenever men continue faithfully to teach the Word of Christ, as they should (John 8:31), then it is Christ Himself who through them performs to this day His prophetic office.

In a wider sense the prophecy of Christ includes the revelation of all the will of God, both Law and Gospel. But the chief part of it is the Gospel, which tells us that Christ saved us through His life and death. Without the prophetic office of Christ no one could know of the grace of God and of the meaning of Christ's life and death. Cf. 1 Corinthians 2:8–11. As our Prophet, Christ makes known and offers to us what He procured for us in His priestly office.

CHRIST AS OUR PRIEST

A priest is one who by means of intercession and sacrifices aims to restore man in the favor of God. He deals with God for and in behalf of man. The priest represents man before God. In the Old Testament days the office of priest existed among the children of Israel: Aaron, Eli, the Levites, and the rest. The Old Testament sacrifices did not in themselves atone for sin. They were a shadow of good things to come and had value and power inasmuch as they prefigured Christ's sacrifice on Calvary; they were symbolical.

Christ is our High Priest. Of Him it is written: "For it was indeed fitting [we had a need] that we should have such a high priest, holy, innocent, unstained, separated from sinners, [four ways of expressing the sinlessness of Christ] and exalted above the heavens [Christ is true God]. He has no need, like those high priests [of the Old Testament days], to offer sacrifices daily, first for His own sins and then for those of the people [because they were sinners as were the people], since He did this once for all when He offered up Himself" (Hebrews 7:26–27). Christ's work of redemption, His sacrifice of Himself on the cross, was not symbolic of any future sacrifice. Christ's sacrifice as our

High Priest has value in itself, tremendous value. When He offered up Himself, Christ was both the priest and the sacrifice. By this one sacrifice Christ procured an eternal redemption for all mankind. Christ "is the propitiation for our sins, and not for ours only but also for the sins of the whole world" (1 John 2:2). Cf. Hebrews 9:12; 10:14.

The work of Christ as our High Priest includes three things. (1) He fulfilled the Law for us. This is called the active obedience of Christ, because He performed perfectly what the moral law required in desire, thought, word, and deed. (2) He sacrificed Himself for us in death. This is called the passive obedience of Christ, because Christ bore, or suffered, our guilt and punishment as the substitute for sinners. (3) Christ still is our advocate with God the Father, where He intercedes and pleads for us. "If anyone does sin, we have an advocate with the Father, Jesus Christ the righteous" (1 John 2:1). Since He made full amends for us by His active and passive obedience, Christ is in a position to plead our cause before God.

The priestly office of Christ is important because, as our Priest, Christ actually procured for us the forgiveness of sins, life, and salvation. Cf. Hebrews 10:14, 18.

CHRIST AS OUR KING

A king is he who has power and authority to rule a country. Ruling is the chief feature of his office. In the Old Testament days the office of king existed among the children of Israel: Saul, David, Solomon, and so on.

Christ, too, is a king. But He is not a worldly king (John 18:36). His kingship and kingdom are far greater than that of any earthly ruler. In speaking of Christ's kingdom it is customary to refer to His kingdom of power, His kingdom of grace, and His kingdom of glory.

As the eternal Son of God, Christ is Lord of all things; He has power in heaven and in earth (Matthew 28:18). Cf. Philippians 2:9–11. All things that exist are put under His feet (Ephesians 1:22). Christ rules this kingdom with supreme almighty power; hence it is called His kingdom of power.

In a special sense Christ is King and Ruler of His Church, the

Christians. By means of the Gospel He wins followers (John 18: 36–37), who believe His Holy Word and lead a godly life. This kingdom is extended and spread in the world by the work of Christians, who confess Christ's name before men and tell the story of His love; this is known as mission work. So all Christians are citizens of this kingdom of Christ, for Christ rules in their hearts, where He has made His abode. Because Christ rules in them with love and grace, this kingdom is called Christ's kingdom of grace. This kingdom will last until the end of days.

Christ is also the King of glory. The kingdom of glory is not on earth but in heaven. Cf. 2 Timothy 4:18. It is called the heavenly kingdom, where Christ has all glory (John 17:24), and where all true believers in Christ, passing through death into the kingdom of heaven, also shall be glorified (Romans 8:18). Of this kingdom there shall be no end.

Christ rules His kingdom of power in the interest of His kingdom of grace, and He rules the kingdom of grace so as to prepare us for the kingdom of glory. Cf. 1 Peter 1:3–5. The work of Christ is a unit, and it revolves around the three kingdoms for the one purpose, which is the salvation of mankind.

HOW IS ALL THIS TO AFFECT US?

Christ wants us to believe His message and to accept Him as our Lord and Savior. Since He redeemed us, we are His "possession" (Ephesians 1:14). "You are not your own" (1 Corinthians 6:19). We belong to God. Therefore we should live unto Christ and do what is pleasing to Him. "He died for all, that those who live might no longer live for themselves but for Him who for their sake died and was raised" (2 Corinthians 5:15). The Christian says with the apostle Paul: "I have been crucified with Christ. It is no longer I who live, but Christ who lives in me. And the life I now live in the flesh I live by faith in the Son of God, who loved me and gave Himself for me" (Galatians 2:20). Whoever truly believes that he is Christ's own will live under God in His kingdom and will serve Him in everlasting righteousness, innocence, and blessedness.

CHAPTER 8

How We Become Christians

"It's time that I turn over a new leaf. I am going to improve my life." From statements like these it appears as though a person could by mere self-determination become a Christian. But it is not so. When they speak thus, people think primarily of their outward behavior and not so much of the attitude of their heart. To be a Christian means more than outward conformance to what is right and ethical. Christianity basically and essentially is a change of heart toward God, which is reflected in the manner of a person's life. Christianity is a conversion to God. No amount of self-determination and autosuggestion can change the natural man's heart-motive.

NATURAL MAN IS HELPLESS

No one can by his own reason or strength believe in Jesus Christ or come to Him. "The natural person does not accept the things of the Spirit of God, for they are folly to him, and he is not able to understand them because they are spiritually discerned" (1 Corinthians 2:14). The unregenerate person, the non-Christian, even at his best, is hostile to the things of God for his salvation. He sees no sense or value in them. A person's estimate of the things of God must proceed from the spiritual side, and it is impossible for man to arrive at such an estimate by himself. There is no spark of spirituality in natural man, and therefore his judgment will insist on the utter senselessness of the Gospel.

The Scriptures state that we all are by nature spiritually blind, dead, and the enemies of God. You "were dead in trespasses and sins" (Ephesians 2:1). Man's natural inclination is toward evil. This shows that he is dead to God, spiritually dead, and that he has no strength to do a spiritual act. To come to Christ and to believe in Him is a spiritual act. "For the intention of man's heart is evil from his youth" (Genesis 8:21). "The mind that is set on the flesh is hostile to God" (Romans 8:7). "For by grace you have been saved through faith. And this is not your own doing" (Ephesians 2:8). Man can as little convert himself or assist in bringing about his conversion as he can create his own life.

The Holy Spirit Works Faith in Man

The Holy Spirit alone can bring us to faith in Christ and impart to us the blessings of redemption, which Christ has won for us. "No one can say 'Jesus is Lord' except in the Holy Spirit" (1 Corinthians 12:3). The acknowledgment that Jesus is our Redeemer is wrought by the power of the Holy Spirit. Faith is "the gift of God" (Ephesians 2:8). "You were washed, you were sanctified, you were justified in the name of the Lord Jesus Christ and by the Spirit of our God" (1 Corinthians 6:11). We are cleansed and made holy in God's sight, regarded righteous because of what Christ did for us, through the working of the Holy Spirit in our hearts.

How Does the Holy Spirit Work Faith in Man?

Faith is worked in man by means of the Gospel, wherein the blessings of Christ's redemptive work are made known and are offered to man.

The written and the spoken Word of the Gospel and the Sacraments are called the Means of Grace, because God's grace is offered and imparted to us through them. God first uses the Law to lead us to know our sins and to feel sorry because of them. "Through the law comes knowledge of sin" (Romans 3:20). In order to have us trust in Christ for the forgiveness of our sins, God employs the Means of Grace. The apostle Paul says: "For I became your father in Christ Jesus through the gospel" (1 Corinthians 4:15). Peter writes:

"You have been born again, not of perishable seed but of imperishable, through the living and abiding word of God" (1 Peter 1:23). We are made Christians by a spiritual birth by means of the imperishable Word of God, which in itself is living and has life-giving power. "So faith comes from hearing, and hearing through the word of Christ" (Romans 10:17). Cf. John 17:20; Titus 3:3–7.

Conversion Not by Coercion

The picture *The Light of the World*, painted by Holman Hunt, shows Christ in a garden at midnight. In His left hand He is holding a lantern, and His right hand is knocking on a heavily paneled door. When the painting was unveiled, an art critic remarked, "Mr. Hunt, you haven't finished your work. There is no handle on that door." "That," said the artist, "is the door to the human heart—it can be opened only from the inside."

"Behold, I stand at the door and knock. If anyone hears My voice and opens the door, I will come in to him and eat with him, and he with Me" (Revelation 3:20).

Conversion is not by compulsion. Christ does not force Himself into man's heart by sheer power. Conversion is not by coercion. Christ moves man to open his heart by having repentance and remission of sins preached in His name. Cf. Luke 24:47. When man "hears Christ's voice," he is by God brought to faith and is made willing and eager to open the door of his heart. It is through the Gospel itself that God exerts His persuasive power. The power of the Holy Spirit is operative in the preaching of the Gospel. So it is Christ who by His Spirit opens the door of man's heart from the inside.

The Meaning of Believing

"To believe in God" means to know, and to accept as true, what the Bible says of God and to trust in Him and to rely on Him with firm confidence. Saving faith is trust in the grace that is offered to us in the Gospel. First of all, it is necessary to learn and to know what we are to believe. Faith and the divine Word are mutually related. "So faith comes from hearing, and hearing through the word of Christ"

(Romans 10:17). A faith without knowledge is an impossibility. All who wish to be saved must know what God has done for their salvation. Furthermore, we must trust in the teachings pertaining to our salvation and have the feeling that they will help and benefit us. Faith is never a bare intellectual knowledge and assent but is an emotional attitude of the heart plus an act of the will. Faith is a knowledge that has affected the heart and will, working the conviction and the confidence that we have grace, righteousness, and forgiveness of sins through Christ. Such confidence Paul expresses: "I know whom I have believed, and I am convinced that He is able to guard until that Day what has been entrusted to me" (2 Timothy 1:12).

Jesus described the Gospel call by means of the parable of the great banquet (Luke 14:16–17), and the parable of the wedding feast (Matthew 22:1–10).

Terms Defined

The work of the Holy Spirit in making us Christians is called conversion or regeneration. It is called "conversion," or "turning," because the Holy Spirit turns us from sin toward our Savior. Cf. Jeremiah 31:18. It is called "regeneration," or "new birth," because a new spiritual life is born in us through the work of the Holy Spirit; we are "created in Christ Jesus" (Ephesians 2:10), and have become "a new creation" (2 Corinthians 5:17).

Conversion Is Instantaneous

The sinner's return to God, that is, his conversion, is effected in the moment when, turning away in despair from his own morality or his own righteousness, he accepts the grace of God offered to him in the Gospel or when he believes the Gospel. "A great number who believed turned to the Lord" (Acts 11:21). One commentator said, "To turn to the Lord means to believe in Christ as our Mediator, through whom we have eternal life." The conversion of man does not consist in his attempting to reform his life or to arouse some sort of "religious" feelings in himself. As soon as a person believes in Christ, even if his faith is but a glimmering spark, his conversion has taken place.

Scripture teaches that man cannot occupy a middle ground between unconverted and converted. Scripture recognizes but two classes of men, believers and unbelievers, or converted and unconverted. The preparation for conversion may extend over a longer or shorter period of time; not so conversion. Only in the sense of "preparation for conversion" may conversion be said to take place gradually. However, conversion in itself is instantaneous and is never a lengthy process.

When the first beginnings of faith and conversion are given to man, there begins at once the struggle of the flesh and the Spirit in him, which indicates that he is spiritually alive or converted. This conflict does not occur without the activity of the will. By the grace of God the will of the believer has been renewed and has been given new powers so that the believer will pray for a stronger faith and will neglect no opportunity for growth in faith and in piety. We Christians should constantly seek to become stronger believers. "Examine yourselves, to see whether you are in the faith. Test yourselves" (2 Corinthians 13:5).

Why Do Not All Heed
the Invitation of the Gospel?

Questions like these arise in the minds of many people: "Why are not all converted who hear the invitation of the Gospel?" "Is there a difference among men?" "Is the attitude of God toward all men the same?"

There is no difference among men; they are all equally unworthy to be converted and saved (2 Timothy 1:9), equally incompetent to convert themselves, and by nature equally unwilling to be converted (1 Corinthians 2:14; 12:3; Ephesians 2:1; Romans 8:7).

There is no difference in the attitude of God toward men. God earnestly would convert and save all men (1 Timothy 2:4), and He alone can convert (1 Corinthians 12:3; Jeremiah 31:18). The Holy Spirit is active, seeking to convert wherever the Gospel is preached.

It would seem to follow that if the same grace of God works wherever the Gospel is being preached, the same effect would result:

all would be converted. Despite the fact that converting grace in every case works with all the power of God, man can still prevent his conversion. "You were not willing" (Matthew 23:37). "You always resist the Holy Spirit" (Acts 7:51). If God worked conversion in an immediate manner (without an intermediary), in His uncovered majesty, man could not resist God. However, man can resist when God operates through means, and God does operate through the means of the Word when He converts man. That does not make God's power less divine and less potent.

We have no right to construct or to develop a doctrine on the basis of our rational deductions but must bring every thought into captivity to the obedience of Christ (2 Corinthians 10:5), and bow in humble submission to the superior wisdom of God. Accordingly, if any man is turned to God in conversion, this is solely and exclusively the work of the Holy Spirit; but if man remains unconverted, it is solely and exclusively man's own fault. Beyond this we must not try to reason.

CONVERSION CHANGES MAN'S ATTITUDE TO GOD AND TO HIS LAW

Faith in Christ changes man's attitude toward God and toward His Law. As faith grows and becomes stronger, and as man's understanding increases, the attitude by the grace of God improves. To the natural man the "things of the Spirit" are "foolishness," but to the convert they become precious wisdom of God. An appreciation of the God-pleasing way of life is given to the believer. Man, who by nature has a carnal mind, which is enmity against God, has by the grace of God through his conversion become a lover of God. His heart is filled with love toward God and toward his neighbor. Accordingly, so far as he is reborn or converted, he will do good works as the commandments of God direct him to do. God is the author of his spiritual life. They to whom He gives spiritual life will abound in good works. The right attitude of the convert springs from the love of God and is the fruit of God's Spirit working in him. God is the unseen source from which the good works spring. A true Christian does not boast of his good works, which are his privilege to perform, knowing that it is the power of Christ and God in him that enables him to follow the example of Christ. "We are His workmanship, created in Christ Jesus for good works" (Ephesians 2:10).

CONVERSION CHANGES
MAN'S PHILOSOPHY OF LIFE

Each person has a philosophy of life; it consists of the principles that underlie his activity; it determines his perspective, governs his viewpoint, measures for him the worth of things. What we think in our hearts makes us the kind of persons we are. "As he calculates in his soul, so is he" (Proverbs 23:7).

A Christian is a "new creation. The old has passed away; behold, the new has come" (2 Corinthians 5:17). Or, as the apostle Paul says at another place: "The life I now live in the flesh I live by faith in the Son of God, who loved me and gave Himself for me" (Galatians 2:20). "For me to live is Christ, and to die is gain" (Philippians 1:21). In these passages we have expressed the Christian's philosophy of life. Jesus came to redeem us from sin, that we might have the right principle of living. Jesus says: "I came that they may have life and have it abundantly" (John 10:10).

We live at our best when we live by the will of God. Christ's philosophy of life for us is based on three fundamental things: (1) that God is good, that He loves sinful mankind even to the point of saving man from perdition through Jesus Christ; (2) that God has a program for our life, namely, that we are to glorify God and seek to win others for God; and (3) that we are to make God's business our first concern in life.

The Christian philosophy of life is thoroughly practical; it involves plain, normal living. It makes for happiness, for it is joy in the Lord. A man experiences the greatest moment of his life when he becomes a Christian.

CHAPTER 9

The Forgiveness of Sins

Of all the blessings that God bestows upon us, none compares in importance with the forgiveness of sins, or the justification of the sinner by faith without the deeds of the Law. Since sin is man's greatest problem, the forgiveness of sins is man's greatest need. The forgiveness of sins is the center of the entire Christian doctrine, for it constitutes the very essence of the Christian religion.

Whoever trusts in his own goodness has no interest in the forgiveness of sins, which Christianity offers to a sinful world. All religions except Christianity teach that man can make amends before the supreme being by deeds of his own, and that there is no gift of forgiveness.

The forgiveness of sins is and remains the source and the basis of all benefits and blessings that man receives from God. He who has the forgiveness of sins has everything. The Scriptures present all other spiritual gifts and activities as resulting from the forgiveness of sins. Truly "blessed is the man against whom the Lord will not count his sin" (Romans 4:8).

To Forgive Sins Is God's Prerogative

The scribes, though unbelieving, correctly asked: "Who can forgive sins but God alone?" (Mark 2:7). Since sin is the transgression of the holy *will of God,* the forgiveness of sins remains a *divine* prerogative. God gave the Law by which human behavior is to be judged. Every violation of that Law is sin. Only God, whose Law has been transgressed, can pardon the transgressor. When God forgives sin, the matter ends right there.

Human Works Cannot Help

The natural man seeks forgiveness for his sin by his own striving and efforts. He regards it foolishness to speak about a free forgiveness from God. He believes that a "moral quality" in man or an "ethical achievement" by man must at least be a contributing factor for forgiveness, if not the entire requirement. But man is wrong.

The Scriptures teach that the forgiveness of sins is not given for any works man has done in the past, or because of anything he may do in the future. The forgiveness of sins does not hinge on any human accomplishment or worthiness. It is altogether independent of any human quality or any "improvement" in man. Honesty, charity, love, kindness, sympathy, friendliness, and other human virtues contribute absolutely nothing toward receiving forgiveness from God. Scripture states: "You are severed from Christ, you who would be justified by the law; you have fallen away from grace" (Galatians 5:4). The forgiveness of sins is obtained only by eliminating the deeds of the Law completely. A sinner cannot make himself right with God and therefore cannot forgive himself. Insofar as the flesh still clings to us, we are affected with the false opinion that forgiveness is by the deeds of the Law. Doing according to the commandments cannot help us. The forgiveness of sin would become uncertain if a single perfect work were necessary.

Forgiveness Is the Gift of God

"For by grace you have been saved through faith. And this is not your own doing; it is *the gift of God*, not a result of works, so that no one may boast" (Ephesians 2:8–9). God forgives our sin not on our account but for Jesus' sake, from sheer grace. The Gospel bids us to receive the forgiveness of sins as a present. God forgives graciously and freely from pure mercy. "We are justified by His grace as a gift, through the redemption that is in Christ Jesus" (Romans 3:24).

MERCY BECAUSE OF CHRIST'S WORK

God is merciful to sinful man because of Christ and His work of redemption. "For our sake He [God] made Him [Jesus] to be sin who knew no sin, so that in Him we might become the righteousness of God" (2 Corinthians 5:21). Christ's one sacrifice has provided all the forgiveness needed. God did not make Jesus to be a sinner, but sin; that is, God laid upon His Son the iniquity of us all (Isaiah 53:6). Jesus was the Lamb of God who took away the sin of the world (John 1:29). Christ, the eternal Son of God, assumed the human nature into His divine being and lived under the Law, which condemns us as sinners. In our place He fulfilled this Law, and in our place He atoned for all our sins by suffering our guilt and punishment. God's love to us rests on Christ's work for us.

THE MEANING OF FORGIVENESS

The forgiveness of sins means that God does not lay to our charge any violation of the Ten Commandments in desire, thought, word, and deed. "In Christ God was reconciling the world to Himself, not counting their trespasses against them" (2 Corinthians 5:19). "Come now, let us reason together, says the LORD: though your sins are like scarlet, they shall be as white as snow; though they are red like crimson, they shall become like wool" (Isaiah 1:18); this is a figurative description of sins being forgiven by God. "Covering sins" is another way in which forgiveness is described. "Blessed are those whose lawless deeds are forgiven, and whose sins are covered" (Romans 4:7). In the place of our sins God has placed the righteousness of our Savior, Jesus Christ.

FORGIVENESS BY WAY OF THE GOSPEL

God does not bestow the forgiveness of sins by some special "internal light" and mysterious revelation. God works neither through silence nor through the shouting and uproar of revivals.

There are certain means by which God works. We call them the Means of Grace, because they offer the grace and love of God. God's Means of Grace are the Word of the Gospel, Baptism, and the Lord's Supper. Each one of these means offers the full remission of sins that Christ provided for us. The assurance of forgiveness in various ways (by reading or hearing the Gospel, by Baptism, by the Lord's Supper) meets the practical need of Christians. Christ says that man "will believe in Me [Christ] through their [apostles'] word" (John 17:20). The Scriptures say that we are regenerated (born again spiritually) by the Word and by Baptism (1 Peter 1:23; Titus 3:5); this means that we have our sins forgiven. The forgiveness of sins is not symbolized by the Gospel but is proclaimed and promised by it.

FORGIVENESS PURCHASED FOR ALL

"In Christ God was reconciling *the world* unto Himself" (2 Corinthians 5:19). Christ has purchased the forgiveness of all sins for all people. If the Gospel excepted but a single person from the grace of God and from the forgiveness of sins, and the name of this unfortunate being were not recorded in the Scriptures, no person could believe, on the basis of the Gospel, that God is gracious and forgiving to him. Thanks be to God that forgiveness is there for all. The reconciliation that God brought about is history, a finished event lying in the past, that pertains to all mankind. "He [Christ] is the propitiation [atonement, appeasement] for our sins, and not for ours only but also for the sins of *the whole world*" (1 John 2:2).

INDIVIDUAL APPROPRIATION BY FAITH

To have the benefit of forgiveness, man must by faith take for himself the promise of forgiveness contained in the Gospel message. Faith is the hand that lays hold of the forgiveness of sins. A gift is offered to be accepted. The free gift of forgiveness and its acceptance by faith go hand in hand, each implying the other. It is God's Spirit who leads us to faith. By faith the believer applies the general promise of forgiveness in the Gospel to himself. Cf. 1 Timothy 2:6; John 1:29; 3:16. With the apostle Paul every Christian declares: "I live *by faith* in the Son of God, who loved me and gave Himself for me" (Galatians 2:20), and with Job: "I *know* that my Redeemer lives" (Job 19:25). Faith in the forgiveness of sins is in every case personal faith. "I believe the forgiveness of sins," confesses the Christian. Faith is the instrument by which the Christian grasps the free gift of God's forgiveness of his sins.

GODLY LIFE IS THE RESULT OF FORGIVENESS

Christian living always appears solely as the result of the forgiveness of sins. The promise of forgiveness is portrayed in the good works of Christians. Good works show and prove to man that inwardly one has accepted the forgiveness of sins offered by the grace of God in the Gospel. Good works are the thank offerings for the forgiveness of sins, which faith has grasped. Peter speaks of this: "Brothers, be all the more diligent to confirm your calling and election" (2 Peter 1:10); he means that by our life we should prove that we believe the forgiveness of sins. Where there is true faith in the forgiveness of sins, there good works surely will follow, for good works flow from faith. In Romans 5:1–5, the apostle Paul declares that the joyous hope of eternal life and patience in tribulation are the fruit of the forgiveness of sins. Again: our being forgiven by God will make us forgiving toward our fellow men. Cf. Matthew 6:12; 18:23–35. Again: only faith in the forgiveness of sins for Christ's sake makes prayer a prayer "in the name of Christ." Again: the knowledge of the forgiveness of sins gives us the comforting hope that we shall not remain in death. The Scriptures teach that all Christian virtues are the result and the effect of faith, which appropriates the forgiveness of sins gained only by the merits of Christ.

LEADS TO ETERNAL SALVATION

"Where there is forgiveness of sins, there is also life and salvation" (Luther's Small Catechism, The Sacrament of the Altar). Christ's promise for a home in heaven is dependent on the forgiveness of sins secured by the redemptive work of Christ. Cf. John 3:16.

PREACH THE FORGIVENESS IN THE WORLD

The apostles were commanded to spread the news of forgiveness through Christ into all the world. That remains the purpose of the Christian Church until the end of time. Christ says: "That repentance and forgiveness of sins should be proclaimed in His [Christ's] name to all nations, beginning from Jerusalem" (Luke 24:47). "And He said to them, 'Go into all the world and proclaim the gospel to the whole creation. Whoever believes and is baptized will be saved, but whoever does not believe will be condemned' " (Mark 16:15–16). To Christians God has given the keys of the kingdom of heaven. It is a wondrous truth to proclaim to the world that God in His heart has forgiven all sins and that He offers this forgiveness in the Gospel, the good news of man's salvation through Christ.

CHAPTER 10

Prayer, the Heartbeat of Faith

Prayer is inseparable from the spiritual life of the child of God; it is the heartbeat of his faith. Whoever has become a child of God desires to speak to his heavenly Father; he prays. "You have received the Spirit of adoption as sons, by whom we cry, 'Abba! Father!' " (Romans 8:15). Through prayer the Christian recognizes and honors God as his helper in every need. Paul, after his conversion, was found in prayer, which was a natural consequence of his having found the Savior. The Christian worships God in prayer.

Prayer is a religious act. Generally considered, it is as natural and as universal as is religion. This universality of prayer-practice is due to man's inborn conviction that there is a Supreme Being who has power to help or to destroy him, and to whom he is accountable. Therefore not everything that bears the name of prayer is God pleasing. Prayer to a false god is idolatry. Only the prayer of the Christian is God pleasing, for only the Christian addresses the true God.

THE FORM OF PRAYER

We may pray by word of mouth, sung or spoken. However, also the thoughts, meditations, and desires of the heart may be prayers. "Let the words of my mouth and the meditation of my heart be acceptable in your sight, O LORD, my rock and my redeemer" (Psalm 19:14). "O LORD, You hear the desire of the afflicted" (Psalm 10:17). Even when not constantly engaged in prayer, Christians are always in the spirit of prayer, for their heart is filled with gratitude to God and trust in Him. Cf. Ephesians 6:18; Romans 8:26–27.

THE CONTENT OF THE CHRISTIAN'S PRAYER

In our prayers we thank and praise God for blessings received, and we ask Him for such things as we need for body and soul. "Do not be anxious about anything [have no cares or worries about anything], but in everything by prayer and supplication with thanksgiving let your requests be made known to God" (Philippians 4:6).

TO WHOM SHOULD WE PRAY?

We should pray only to the true God, Father, Son, and Holy Spirit, since to Him alone such honor is due and since He alone is able and willing to hear us and to grant our prayer. Prayers to any other except the true God, no matter how sincerely spoken or thought, are a form of idolatry and are vain. Cf. 1 Kings 18:25–29. Saints cannot hear our prayers (Isaiah 63:16), and angels do not merit worship (Revelation 22:8–9). While praying to the true God, we need not mention all three persons of the Trinity, since they are united in one divine essence.

THE BASIS OF CHRISTIAN PRAYER

Faith in the love of God in Christ Jesus is basic to Christian prayer. Only when we trust in the merits of the Savior will our prayers touch the heart of God. Before a person can truly pray to God, he must by faith in Christ have entered into the right relationship with God. "Therefore, since we have been justified by faith, we have peace with God through our Lord Jesus Christ. Through Him we have also obtained access by faith into this grace in which we stand, and we rejoice in hope of the glory of God" (Romans 5:1–2). Cf. Romans 10:14. Therefore Jesus says: "Whatever you ask of the Father in My name, He will give it to you" (John 16:23).

MOTIVES FOR PRAYER

God's command and promise, our own and our neighbor's need, and gratitude for blessings received should move us to pray. Because of the Christian's childlike relation to God, he is moved for these reasons freely and joyfully to express his worship of God in prayer.

God's gracious invitation is "Seek My face" (Psalm 27:8). Again, "Call upon Me in the day of trouble" (50:15). God promises to hear us. "Ask, and it will be given to you; seek, and you will find; knock, and it will be opened to you. For everyone who asks receives, and the one who seeks finds, and to the one who knocks it will be opened" (Matthew 7:7–8). Cf. Psalm 50:15; 145:18–19. Our own and our neighbor's trouble and need should move us to pray. It is not a weakness to bring our troubles to God. Cf. Isaiah 26:16; Luke 17:13; 18:13. We should also thank God for what He has done for us in answer to our prayers or even without our prayers. Having delivered us, God wants us to glorify Him. Cf. Luke 17:15–18.

What May We Ask for in Prayer?

In prayer we may ask for everything that adds to the glory of God and to our own and our neighbor's welfare, both spiritual and bodily things. Cf. Mark 11:24; Philippians 4:6. All prayers must be in agreement with the will of God if they are to be answered. "This is the confidence that we have toward Him, that if we ask anything according to His will He hears us" (1 John 5:14).

When praying for spiritual blessings, necessary for our salvation and for living a Christian life, we should ask unconditionally, or without reservation, since such requests are always in accord with the will of God. When praying for specific earthly things, which God has not specifically promised, we must leave it to God's will and wisdom; and therefore we should in these matters pray conditionally, the condition being that it is good for us; that will be according to God's will. Cf. Luke 11:13; 22:42.

How Should We Pray?

We should pray with a firm faith in Christ as our Redeemer, and with confidence that for His sake our prayers will be answered. This requires a thoughtful, sincere action; we are to think of what we are saying, and we must mean what we say. We are to pray with penitent hearts, lifting up "holy hands without anger or quarreling" (1 Timothy 2:8). We should not permit doubt to nullify our prayers. "But let him ask in faith, with no doubting, for the one who doubts is like a wave of the sea that is driven and tossed by the wind. For that person must not suppose that he will receive anything from the Lord" (James 1:6–7). We should with confidence approach God, because He has promised to hear us. "And whatever you ask in prayer, you will receive, if you have faith" (Matthew 21:22). Cf. John 16:23.

Proper Prayers Are Answered

God answers every proper prayer but in His own way and at His own time. Our prayers may not always be answered in the way we ask or expect but certainly in a way that is best for us. The apostle Paul's prayer was answered in his best interest. Cf. 2 Corinthians 12:8–9. Jesus did not at once grant the request of the Canaanite woman but held back to test her faith, eventually helping her. Cf. Matthew 15:22–28. Thus it may seem that for "a small moment" God has forsaken us and "hid His face" from us, but with everlasting kindness will He have mercy on us (Isaiah 54:7–8). Therefore we should never be discouraged when our prayers are not answered immediately, but we should continue to call with all confidence, to "be constant in prayer" (Romans 12:12); and when His hour comes, God will answer our prayer. God's delays are not denials. His answer may be different from what we have in mind, and His time schedule may not agree with ours. However, God will answer every proper prayer.

For Whom Should We Pray?

We should pray for ourselves and for all other people, even for our enemies. "First of all, then, I urge that supplications, prayers, intercessions, and thanksgivings be made for all people" (1 Timothy 2:1). "Pray for those who persecute you" (Matthew 5:44). The tax collector prayed for himself (Luke 18:13). Abraham prayed for the city of Sodom (Genesis 18:23–32). The Canaanite woman prayed for her daughter (Matthew 15:22–28). Jesus prayed for His enemies (Luke 23:34); likewise did Stephen (Acts 7:60).

We should not pray for the souls of the dead, since God has neither commanded it, nor has He promised to hear such prayers. Besides, it is altogether useless, for after death there is judgment. Cf. Hebrews 9:27.

OUR SECRET SUPPORT

It is a privilege to have friends who will go up into the mount of prayer and plead with God in our behalf. Moses did this for Israel, who sinned against God. When we note the results of this prayer for Israel, we see a very great power of intercession. The wrath of God was stayed.

We cannot know what blessings come to us and what woes and penalties are averted from us through the intercession of friends. No duty of love is more sacred than that of praying for those we love. Especially should we pray for them if they have sinned, that they may repent and be forgiven. Not to make intercession for them is to close an important avenue of love and help. Let us never forget what riches we can give to our fellow men through a word to God in their interest. Prayer is a secret but powerful support.

PLACES OF PRAYER

Prayers need not be confined to any particular building or to supposedly holy localities. The sanctity of a place does not add value or strength to our prayers. We should pray everywhere (1 Timothy 2:8), especially in private, that is, when we are alone (Matthew 6:6). Christ often withdrew from the multitude to be alone with God in prayer (Luke 5:16). We should also pray in the family circle, at table, in the family devotion, and in public worship. "In the great assembly I will bless the LORD" (Psalm 26:12). Cf. Acts 1:14; 2:42.

The Jews' Wailing Wall

On the west side of the temple area in Jerusalem there is a celebrated stretch of ancient masonry 156 feet in length by 59 feet in height, known as the Jews' Wailing Wall. Every Friday afternoon about four o'clock multitudes of Jews assemble and, with tears in their eyes, solemnly repeat the 79th Psalm and the Lamentations of Jeremiah, and pray for the restoration of the temple. It is a touching sight to watch them, as they lean against the weather-beaten wall and kiss and caress the blocks, sometimes tucking in between the stones old rags and pieces of paper on which are inscribed their vows and petitions. This custom has been carried on without interruption for many centuries. These people attach particular significance to the place of their prayers, which in itself is contrary to the Scriptures. However, worse yet is the fact that they do not accept Christ as the Redeemer from sin.

POSTURE AND TIMES OF PRAYER

The Bible prescribes no particular posture that is to be used in prayer. Lifting up hands heavenward was customary in the olden days. We usually fold our hands and bow our heads, or we kneel, to show that we humbly acknowledge our unworthiness of whatever the good Lord may see fit to give us. The Scriptures nowhere restrict us as to times for prayer. When the Scriptures say, "Pray without ceasing" (1 Thessalonians 5:17), they mean that our hearts should always be in the spirit of prayer. It is well to cultivate the habit of prayer at stated times. To pray when we arise in the morning, when we retire at night, when we are at table to eat, when we must make a decision at a critical moment, and so on, is a good custom. Prayer should be the key of the day and the lock of the night.

THE VALUE AND POWER OF PRAYER

Some have said that the value of prayer is strictly psychological and exists only in the mind of him that prays, making him feel that God will help him. Now it is true that prayer has this reassuring effect on our troubled hearts. But the reason for this is that God has promised to hear our prayers. God "fulfills the desire of those who fear Him; He also hears their cry and saves them" (Psalm 145:19). It is for this reason that "prayer of a righteous person has great power" (James 5:16). Prayer does not work like an opiate, having no other effect than to quiet the troubled heart of him who prays. God actually answers prayer. In prayer we call upon the living God, who is able and willing to help us.

Prayer does not justify us before God, for it is a part of the Christian's sanctified life. Prayer is a work in which we engage; and no work in which we are engaged can justify us before God. It is an outgrowth, the result of being a Christian. Prayer is the free and joyful expression of the Christian's childlike relation to God. Through prayer we do not merit, or earn, anything from God. Prayer is not a Means of Grace. Prayer is the blessed privilege of Christians to commune with God. We deprive ourselves of God's blessings by being neglectful of this privilege. "You do not have, because you do not ask" (James 4:2). If we meet the conditions of prayer that God has set, we shall receive God's answer to our prayers.

THE LORD'S PRAYER

The most excellent of all prayers is the Lord's Prayer, taught by the Lord Himself (Matthew 6:9–13; Luke 11:2–4). This prayer may be divided into the introduction, the seven petitions (prayers), and the conclusion.

"Our Father who art in heaven." This has been called "the golden gate of prayer." As His children we should come to God in simplicity, with childlike confidence, with unquestioning trust, and with yearning love. Our heavenly Father withholds nothing from His children that is really good. His ability is unlimited, and His love to us is constant. Cf. 1 John 3:1; Ephesians 3:20; Luke 11:13.

"Hallowed be Thy name." "To hallow" means "to honor, to regard, to keep as something holy." Here we ask God that His name be regarded holy among us by the pure teaching of His Word and by a godly life. We ask that God may bestow upon us the power that in our every act and behavior, in our whole character and influence, we believe and live as His children. Cf. Matthew 5:16. May we so live that others will be able to tell by our attitude and life that we belong to God!

"Thy kingdom come." In this prayer we implore God to dwell in our heart, to rule our life completely, and in time to take us into His

kingdom of glory in heaven. Cf. Colossians 2:6. We also pray that God would extend His kingdom to include men, women, and children everywhere. This is the mission prayer. Cf. 2 Thessalonians 3:1; Matthew 9:38; Acts 4:24–30.

"Thy will be done on earth as it is in heaven." The good and gracious will of God pertains to our salvation and the salvation of others. To that end His name is to be hallowed and His kingdom is to come among men. This prayer includes that everything God wants to do for us according to His promise be done, and that everything God wants us to do and to avoid according to His will be done, and that we endure whatever cross God in His wisdom and love may place upon us during our life. Here we ask that we be saved (1 Timothy 2:4), that we live the Christian life (1 Thessalonians 4:3), and that we deny ourselves and take up our cross and follow Him (Matthew 16:24). To that end may we have strength and perseverance to withstand the evil counsel and will of the devil, the world, and our own flesh. Cf. 1 Peter 5:8, 9; 1 John 2:15–17; Psalm 119:35; 2 Corinthians 12:9.

"Give us this day our daily bread." In this petition we ask God to supply us with what we need for the support and wants of the body and with the necessary material and physical things of this world. God wants us to be satisfied in having what is sufficient for meeting the needs of each day. We are to know the lesson of continual dependence and that we live by the day. Cf. Psalm 145:15; Matthew 6:33–34; Proverbs 30:7–9; 1 Timothy 6:8.

"And forgive us our trespasses, as we forgive those who trespass against us." The first part of this petition is not hard to pray, for we daily sin much and are daily in need of God's forgiveness, which He readily grants to all who come to Him trusting in Jesus' work of redemption. Cf. Luke 15:21; 18:13; Psalm 19:12. But the second part of this petition is not so easy, for our evil flesh is resentful and bitter against those who wrong us. Unless God's love leads us, we will not be forgiving. After we experience God's forgiveness, we will mercifully forgive our neighbor. Our forgiveness of others is the fruit of God's forgiveness. This spirit must never be lacking in us. So we ask God that we may have a forgiving spirit in our heart toward all who wrong us and that we will not be resentful. Blessing and duty are inseparably

linked together in this prayer. God means that if we will not forgive those who wronged us, it is evident that we do not have the true spirit of repentance toward Him with regard to our sins against Him, and so God will not forgive us our sins because of our spirit. Cf. Matthew 18:21–22; Mark 11:25–26; Luke 6:36–37; Ephesians 4:32. To illustrate this petition, we have a parable spoken by Jesus, wherein a wicked servant would not forgive his fellow servant a small debt, while the king was willing to forgive this wicked servant an immense debt (Matthew 18:23–35). Aside from asking God's forgiveness in this petition, we have here a reminder to be forgiving to our fellow men.

"And lead us not into temptation." Here we ask God to strengthen and preserve us whenever any temptation to evil comes upon us. Included herein is the request for good judgment on our part, that in order to avoid the commission of sin, we will also avoid its occasions. Be resolved to go only where duty calls; if we meet temptation there, God will help us from evil if we earnestly beseech Him in prayer to do so. "Let no one say when he is tempted, 'I am being tempted by God,' for God cannot be tempted with evil, and He Himself tempts no one. But each person is tempted when he is lured and enticed by his own desire" (James 1:13–14). "But the Lord is faithful. He will establish you and guard you against the evil one" (2 Thessalonians 3:3). Cf. 1 Corinthians 10:13; Ephesians 6:13.

"But deliver us from evil." We pray in this petition that God would deliver us from all evils of body and soul and in time take us to heaven. We ask God for a blessed death, which delivers us from all the evils men suffer because of their sinfulness. Here achievement of the great objective of life is prayed for. Life on earth is but a pilgrimage. Heaven is the Christian's home. This we seek and desire and pray for. "The Lord will rescue me from every evil deed and bring me safely into His heavenly kingdom" (2 Timothy 4:18). "I am hard pressed between the two. My desire is to depart and be with Christ, for that is far better" (Philippians 1:23).

"For Thine is the kingdom and the power and the glory forever and ever. Amen." In the conclusion the reason is given why we address these seven petitions to God. Human helpers fail us, but our heavenly Father is the everlasting King, who alone has power to answer

our prayers, and to whom alone all glory and praise should be given. "Amen" means "it shall be so" or "so be it"; it expresses our firm assurance that God will grant these petitions.

CHAPTER 11

The Symphony of Life

Once, when Sir Michael Costa was having rehearsal with a vast array of performers and hundreds of voices, the man who played the piccolo, far off in some corner, said within himself, "In all this noise nobody can hear me," and so he ceased to play. Suddenly the great conductor stopped, flung up his hands, and all was still; and then he cried aloud, "Where is the piccolo?" The quick ear missed it, and all was spoiled because it failed to take its part.

Followers of Jesus have a part to play in the symphony of life. How often we feel like that piccolo player, thinking our small efforts and expended energies are of no avail, and that the family, the community, the church, can well do without our services. So we cease to play our part. Yet there is One who listens to it. Until we are relieved from services by Him, we have a part to play in which He is interested.

We may not be shouldering exceptionally high responsibilities. Our appointed tasks may seem of little value in the great symphony of the Christian life. Yet all the music of God's universe is made richer and sweeter because of the harmony supplied by individuals, each one seemingly unimportant alone, yet highly valuable in ensemble with fellow humans.

Whether our abilities be large or small, the important thing is to use them to glorify our Savior on our earthly pilgrimage. The result is a God-pleasing life. With the psalmist let us say: "Your statutes [God's laws] have been my songs [my way of living] in the house of my sojourning [during my life on earth]" (Psalm 119:54).

CHRISTIANS ARE STEWARDS OF GOD

The word *steward* clearly expresses the place God has assigned to us in our relationship to Him. A steward is one to whom something has been entrusted for care and use. He does not own what has been entrusted to him. He is working altogether in his master's interests. A steward is a responsible partner of the master in the carrying out of the master's purpose. God wants us to administer our whole life in accordance with His will and in harmony with the spirit and ideals of Christ. "Have this mind among yourselves, which is yours in Christ Jesus" (Philippians 2:5). Stewardship is the investment of our whole life for God. We are not our own. We belong to God.

Because we Christians are the instruments of God and the children of the heavenly Father, Christ says to us: "You are the salt of the earth. . . . You are the light of the world" (Matthew 5:13–14). Since we have accepted the Lord Jesus Christ with our whole heart, we say with the apostle Paul: "For me to live is Christ" (Philippians 1:21). "For none of us lives to himself, and none of us dies to himself. For if we live, we live to the Lord, and if we die, we die to the Lord. So then, whether we live or whether we die, we are the Lord's" (Romans 14:7–8). In all things we are to live unto the Lord. "So, whether you eat or drink, or whatever you do, do all to the glory of God" (1 Corinthians 10:31).

Christian stewardship properly describes the life of the Christian. The Christian's "delight is in the law of the Lord" (Psalm 1:2). As he loves God, he is willing to do what pleases God. "I delight to do your will, O my God; Your law is within my heart" (Psalm 40:8). Stewardship has been aptly defined as "the practice of the Christian religion."

STEWARDSHIP OF OUR SOCIAL CONTACTS

God made man a social creature. We are important to one another. Our interdependence carries with it great responsibilities. God recognizes this responsibility and therefore gave us this commandment: "You shall love your neighbor as yourself" (Mark 12:31). To each one of us God has assigned a definite place and sphere of influence. The Second Table of the Law tells us in detail how our love to our neighbor should be expressed. The apostle Paul speaks of the stewardship of social contacts: "I am under obligation both to Greeks and to barbarians, both to the wise and to the foolish" (Romans 1:14). In Romans 12, we have definite and specific instructions regarding our behavior toward our fellow men. "And this commandment we have from Him: whoever loves God must also love his brother" (1 John 4:21).

STEWARDS OF OUR TIME

As creatures of God and redeemed of the Lord we have to give an account to God of the use we are making of our allotted time on earth. Christ is the Lord of our time.

Time on earth is a prelude to eternity. Our lifetime is a probation period during which we are to learn to know God and to live according to His will. Christians pray to God: "So teach us to number our days that we may get a heart of wisdom" (Psalm 90:12). All our time is seedtime. We are constantly sowing our thoughts, words, and deeds. "For the one who sows to his own flesh will from the flesh reap corruption, but the one who sows to the Spirit will from the Spirit reap eternal life" (Galatians 6:8). "Whoever sows sparingly will also reap sparingly, and whoever sows bountifully will also reap bountifully" (2 Corinthians 9:6). The type of sowing determines the manner in which we use our time; it shows whether we fulfill God's purpose or not.

To make the most of our time requires good planning. Proper planning calls for the proper balance between the various duties of life; all should receive their proper place, attention, and effort. A right balance must be kept between our spiritual and our secular duties. There must be time for the worship of God, for meditation on the goodness of God, for prayer, for church services, for personal service in the church. "Seek first the kingdom of God and His righteousness" (Matthew 6:33). There must be time for the pursuit of our earthly calling, or vocation, and the duties involved therewith. Cf. Genesis 2:15; 2 Thessalonians 3:10. There must be time for rest and relaxation. It is not good for the bow always to be bent. It is poor stewardship of time to burn the candle at both ends. "Look carefully then how you walk, not as unwise but as wise, making the best use of the time, because the days are evil" (Ephesians 5:15–16). Jesus urges us: "We must work the works of him who sent me while it is day; night is coming, when no one can work" (John 9:4).

Principles to Govern Us
in Acquiring Possessions

Man was made for labor. The wonderful physical and mental endowments which were his in creation were given him for useful employment. To work with brain and muscle is God's arrangement for man. "By the sweat of your face you shall eat bread, till you return to the ground" (Genesis 3:19). In his natural life man owes it to God, to himself, and to his fellow human beings to work and to be constructively busy. In this matter we must guard against a selfish spirit, which is a strong motive prompted by our old Adam. Our diligence must be motivated by principles of Christian stewardship.

Because of Christ's love for us we are to show a sense of love and justice in following our trade or profession, and we are to use only honorable ways of coming into the possession of material goods. We will be engaged in useful work, beneficial to society, and will take into account our particular talents and tastes, with which God has wisely endowed us.

The Bible lays down no specific laws regarding the amount of material possessions we might hold. Jesus never idealized poverty nor did He condemn wealth. However, He did issue emphatic warnings against the danger of riches, for He knew that with man "the love of money is the root of all kinds of evils" (1 Timothy 6:10). We should be content to have sufficient goods to take care of our personal needs and of our opportunities for service. Two things we ought to remember. The first is that persons are more precious than property; we may possess *things,* but should not let things possess *us.* The second is that so-called property rights are purely relative; we are not the absolute owners. The rights of God and of our fellow men must be considered and regarded. God wants to know how we acquire money and goods before He asks us how we use them. "One's life does not consist in the abundance of his possessions" (Luke 12:15).

PRINCIPLES TO GOVERN
THE USE OF OUR POSSESSIONS

It really is easier to make money and to acquire possessions than it is to use the acquired materials wisely. The Bible says: "Honor the Lord with your wealth and with the firstfruits of all your produce" (Proverbs 3:9). By the use of our possessions we express ourselves, our ideals, our soul life, just as we do by our words and acts. Such expression may be for better or for worse. Money talks; it talks about us. The Christian will use his material possessions as an expression of his converted self. He believes that "As each has received a gift, use it to serve one another, as good stewards of God's varied grace" (1 Peter 4:10). A love of God and man is the only right motive for the proper administration of our money and material goods. Cf. 1 Corinthians 13:3. Directly or indirectly all things should be used to the honor of God.

SEVEN MAJOR NEEDS IN LIFE

The seven major needs in life are shelter, food and clothing, education, business, government, recreation, and religion. Around these seven needs practically all activities of the human race revolve. The needs may be classified as being of physical, intellectual, and spiritual natures.

Just how much or in what proportion we are to use our material possessions to satisfy these seven needs is nowhere indicated in the Bible. In some respects the urgency and the amount necessary vary with different people. It depends on the weight of obligation. We are always to use good judgment, however, and should not permit luxuries to be regarded as necessities.

Our religion deserves first consideration because it is basic to all other needs in life. God says so in the Law, for the First Commandment is basic to all other commandments. Some of the Christian's possessions are to be administered directly for the cause of his religion. This applies also to the use of talents as they may be of value. We are to use the Church for our own sake and for the sake of bringing others under its blessed influence. In this respect there should be a constant striving for higher and better standards in every Christian life.

BEING ALL THERE

One reason why we often accomplish so little is that we do not organize our talents. The lack of being all there in interest, in energy, and in application usually is the cause of an unfruitful life. Solomon exhorts us: "Whatever your hand finds to do, do it with your might" (Ecclesiastes 9:10).

In one of the laboratories of Washington there is a great sunglass measuring three feet across. It gathers the rays of the sun that strike its flat surface and focuses them on a single point a few feet below. At this point a terrible heat is created, which cannot be measured. All this is but three feet of ordinary sunshine concentrated on a single point. Scattered, these rays are hardly felt; concentrated, they melt adamant.

We are to begin all our undertakings in the name of the Lord. When we do that and focus our energies on the task at hand, we can do seemingly tremendous things. God blesses our efforts if they really are efforts.

By being all there, we shall not waste energy, but, on the contrary, we shall actually conserve it. We shall be surprised at what we really can do if we make sincere efforts. The result is not only worthwhile accomplishment but also increased self-confidence and courage to meet additional problems and duties of life.

GOD REWARDS FAITHFUL STEWARDS

A faithful life of Christian stewardship will not go unrewarded. Faithfulness to God according to our individual abilities has its compensations. In this life God will increase our abilities and opportunities to serve Him, and in the life to come we shall by the grace of God inherit the kingdom prepared for us in heaven.

CHAPTER 12

The Law,
Guide to Christian Behavior

The Christian desires to do what pleases God. He has learned to know and to appreciate the love of God, and so his own heart is filled with love and gratitude to God. "We love because He first loved us" (1 John 4:19). This change of heart, also called "the new obedience," will invariably show itself in a change of behavior in life. Conversion by the Holy Spirit renews man's heart so that he can now overcome sin and do good works before God. "Those who belong to Christ Jesus have crucified the flesh with its passions and desires" (Galatians 5:24). The Christian will resist temptation and the devil by means of his faith (1 Peter 5:9). And though here and there he fall into sin, he will not let sin rule over him (Romans 6:12). Also in a positive way will he show this change of heart. "We are His workmanship, created in Christ Jesus for good works, which God prepared beforehand, that we should walk in them" (Ephesians 2:10). That we should be zealous in good works is one of the purposes for which Christ redeemed us (Titus 2:14) and for which the Holy Spirit converted us. As the redeemed of the Lord we are to dedicate our lives to the service of God by living before Him in righteousness and holiness. "For this is the will of God, your sanctification" (1 Thessalonians 4:3). It is God's will and our privilege to do according to His commandments.

If we would have peace and happiness in our Christian religion, we must see that we are laborers in the Lord's vineyard. All of us are called into the kingdom of God to work. He who by the grace of God would leave footprints in the sands of time will have to wear work shoes.

Be Good for Something

There is a story of a friar who was eager to show his appreciation to God by illustrating the pages of the Book of Revelation with pictures. He became so absorbed that he neglected the poor and the sick, who were suffering and dying in the plague. When he at last came to the painting of the face of the Lord in the glory of His second coming, his hand had lost its skill. He wondered why, and upon reflecting, he realized that it was because he had neglected his duty in serving his fellow men.

Humiliated by the discovery, the friar went among the sick and dying to minister to their needs. He labored on untiringly, until he himself was smitten with the fatal plague. Then he tottered back to his cell to finish his loved work before he died. He knelt in prayer to ask help, when, behold, he saw that an angel's hand had completed the picture.

This is only a legend, but its lesson is well worth our serious thought. The monk could not paint the face of the Lord while he was neglecting those who needed his ministrations. Nor is the face of the Master painted in full beauty on our souls while we are neglecting any service of love. Not only are we to be good people, but we are to show the positive virtues in Christian service. "Through love serve one another" (Galatians 5:13). It takes service to fill up the measure of the stature of Christ. Let us not simply be good; let us be good for something—good for service to our fellow men who are in need of our love. We should always remember that we are doing this for Christ's sake and in His name.

More Than Outward Conformity Demanded

We must differentiate between works that appear good before man and works that are good before God. God often disapproves what man regards as praiseworthy, and man often ignores and despises what is good and acceptable in the sight of God. Much in this world that appears to be good is so only as far as appearances go, and is not regarded good by God. "Man looks on the outward appearance, but the LORD looks on the heart" (1 Samuel 16:7). The right motive of the heart determines whether any act according to God's command-ments is God pleasing.

THE TWO QUALIFICATIONS OF GOOD WORKS

To be a good work in the sight of God, an act must conform to God's Law, and it must proceed from Christian love. God's Law is the only standard of good works. "You shall be careful therefore to do as the Lord your God has commanded you. You shall not turn aside to the right hand or to the left" (Deuteronomy 5:32). "Blessed is the man who walks not in the counsel of the wicked, nor stands in the way of sinners, nor sits in the seat of scoffers; but his delight is in the law of the Lord, and on his law he meditates day and night. He is like a tree planted by streams of water that yields its fruit in its season" (Psalm 1:1–3). The life of the Christian is not to be governed by what is in vogue or by what others do, but by what is right before God. "In vain do they worship Me, teaching as doctrines the commandments of men" (Matthew 15:9). The second qualification of a good work is that it must proceed from a love of God. Works done according to the Law are not truly good works if done under duress or because they are commanded or if they are done from fear of punishment or from a desire for reward. The alms and prayers of the Pharisees did not please God because they were prompted by vainglory and self-righteousness. Cf. Matthew 6:1–5. "Faith working through love" (Galatians 5:6), and "love is the fulfilling of the law" (Romans 13:10). Cf. Matthew 22:36–40; 1 John 5:3.

THE GOOD WORKS OF THE HEATHEN

Because it is the right attitude of the heart to God which deter-mines the quality and value of a good work, the non-Christian cannot possibly do a spiritually good work before God. The good works of the heathen, or the non-Christian, belong in the sphere of civil righteousness or of the state. In this sphere they deserve high praise, and God rewards the heathen in this life with temporal blessings because of their civil righteousness. The glory and the value of the good works of non-Christians in the civil domain is this, that they are the mainstay of the kingdoms of this world, which by God's will are maintained as the scaffolding for the building of the church. Civil righteousness also is the foundation of the well-being of the community and the state (1 Timothy 2:1-2; Romans 13:1-4). But as to their value in the spiritual sphere, the good works of non-Christians are to be rated as sin, since they are prompted by self-glory. Without any limitations the Scriptures declare that the heathen are dead in sins (Ephesians 2:1), alienated from the life of God (Ephesians 4:18), that they have no hope and are without God in the world (Ephesians 2:12), are carried away unto dumb idols (1 Corinthians 12:2), and that their sacrifices are offered to the devils, not to God (1 Corinthians 10:20). The works of the heathen are good in the civil sphere, but have no spiritual value. For example, an atheist who built a hospital for poor children did an excellent work. But it was not a good work in the sight of God, because no one can do a work intrinsically good until he has been born again, or become a Christian. "Without faith it is impossible to please Him" (Hebrews 11:6). The world says: "It does not so much matter what you believe, just so you live right. It's deeds that count, not creeds." But the Bible teaches that a God-pleasing life is the inevitable expression of faith in God's Word. Faith is active in holiness of heart and in deeds of love. Jesus says: "For I tell you, unless your righteousness exceeds that of the scribes and Pharisees, you will never enter the kingdom of heaven" (Matthew 5:20).

CHRISTIANS ARE NOT PERFECT DOERS
OF THE LAW

Not even Christians can keep the Law of God as God demands it be kept. They still possess the evil nature, the old Adam, and whatever proceeds from this influence is wicked and sinful. The apostle Paul, a Christian, admitted that he was not yet perfect, but that he was unceasingly striving after that perfection which Christ wanted him to have (Philippians 3:12). Cf. Romans 7:14-23. Only as we live in the Spirit shall we walk in the Spirit (Galatians 5:25). All the good works of Christians are tainted with sin, because they are more or less contaminated with the selfishness of the flesh and are motivated by servile fear. However, for Jesus' sake even these imperfect spiritual sacrifices of God's children are acceptable to God. "You yourselves like living stones are being built up as a spiritual house, to be a holy priesthood, to offer spiritual sacrifices acceptable to God through Jesus Christ" (1 Peter 2:5).

BE WILLING TO LEARN

Before an audience that taxed the capacity of a large auditorium a brilliant young musician stepped up buoyantly. Thousands of faces were tense with interest and admiration. The young virtuoso seated himself at the instrument and, as if by magic, charmed his hearers. No music was before him, and his fingers seemed to drop to the keys without effort. The audience marveled. "I wish I could play like that!" was the exclamation of more than one. Most people, however, do not take into account the endless hours of application and practice on scales and finger exercises—the price of being a great musician.

A willingness to learn must be a part of every Christian's program, if one is to grow and develop. We should with all diligence pursue the way to heaven and constantly endeavor to improve our life. There is always room for improvement. We can always be better than we are. But we must want to grow.

It is important that we get our instruction at the right source. We are to learn from God, for He alone can teach us the truth in which we are to walk. "Teach me Your way, O Lord, that I may walk in Your truth; unite my heart to fear Your name" (Psalm 86:11).

TO WHAT EXTENT
ARE GOOD WORKS NECESSARY?

Good works are not necessary for our salvation, for "one is justified by faith apart from works of the law" (Romans 3:28). Good works, however, are necessary as the expression of faith in our hearts. "Faith working though love" (Galatians 5:6). "Faith by itself, if it does not have works, is dead" (James 2:17). "Let your light shine before others, so that they may see your good works and give glory to your Father who is in heaven" (Matthew 5:16). Christ "gave Himself for us to redeem us from all lawlessness and to purify for Himself a people for His own possession who are zealous for good works" (Titus 2:14). Good works are the necessary fruit of repentance (Matthew 3:8), the inevitable product of faith. "Whoever abides in Me and I in him, he it is that bears much fruit, for apart from Me you can do nothing" (John 15:5).

God Promises a Gracious Reward for Christian Behavior

God will graciously reward in body and soul all those who love Him and keep His commandments. The man who makes it his object to do his whole duty according to the Law of God takes the course that is best suited to promote his own highest good here and hereafter. "Godliness is of value in every way, as it holds promise for the present life and also for the life to come" (1 Timothy 4:8). Therefore God says: "Showing steadfast love to thousands of those who love Me and keep My commandments" (Exodus 20:6). On earth this reward may be special blessings easily recognized, or guidance in life which, though not immediately apparent, will result in our welfare. Cf. Ecclesiastes 11:1; Proverbs 19:17. In heaven the reward will consist of a greater degree of glory. "Your reward is great in heaven" (Matthew 5:12). "You will be repaid at the resurrection of the just" (Luke 14:14). Cf. Matthew 25:14–30; Luke 19:12–26; 1 Corinthians 3:12–15. "Whoever sows sparingly will also reap sparingly, and whoever sows bountifully will also reap bountifully" (2 Corinthians 9:6). All these rewards are gifts of God, made to us because of Christ's perfect obedience to the Law, which we in faith accept as our righteousness before God.

Lasting Impressions

Many years ago a beautiful fern grew in a deep vale, nodding in the breeze. One day it fell, believing as it sank away that no one would remember its grace and beauty. Years later a geologist went out with his hammer in the interest of his science. He struck a rock; and there in the seam lay the form of a fern—every leaf, every fiber, the most delicate traceries of the leaves imprinted in the sides of the cleft. It was the fern that ages before grew and dropped into the indistinguishable mass of vegetation. It perished; but its memorial was preserved and today is made manifest.

So it is with the stories of all beautiful lives which have wrought for God and man and have vanished from the earth. Only a few names of the good and the useful in every age are preserved. The great multitude are forgotten. Earth keeps scant record of her benefactors. But there is a place where every kindness, be it ever so small, done in the name of Christ, is recorded and remembered. Nothing is lost; nothing is forgotten. The memorials are in other lives, and someday every touch and trace and influence and impression will be revealed. The acts of worthy lives are cut deep in the eternal rock, where all eyes shall see them forever.

Our every act will in some shape or form affect the life and manner of others. Be it ever so insignificant, it nevertheless makes lasting impressions.

LET US FOLLOW AFTER

The Ten Commandments are the Christian's guide to an exemplary life. They show us the pattern of life which is pleasing to God. With the apostle Paul we "follow after" (Philippians 3:12), seeking ever better to meet the Law's demands. When we fail and fail again to fulfill the requirements of love according to the Law, let us again and again look to Calvary, where the Savior with all His heart and soul and mind loved us even unto death and atoned for our sins. When we do that, we shall by God's grace through His Spirit receive the assurance of the forgiveness of our sins, and we shall be empowered to improve our life according to our heavenly Father's will. When our love to God is right, our love to one another will be right too. "I am the vine; you are the branches. Whoever abides in Me and I in him, he it is that bears much fruit, for apart from Me you can do nothing," says Christ (John 15:5). So we earnestly pray: "Lead me in the path of Your commandments, for I delight in it" (Psalm 119:35). To love God above all things and to love our neighbor as ourselves, we must first have the redeeming love of Christ in our hearts. Let us always view the Law as the guide to Christian behavior in the light of the cross of Christ!

CHAPTER 13

The Christian's Cross and Affliction

One of the insoluble problems of the Christian life is the fact that, on the one hand, the Christians by their faith in Christ enjoy the full favor of God, while, on the other hand, God ordains that this full favor of God should not become manifest in this life. The same lowliness that characterized the earthly life of Christ is to characterize the life of the Christian. "Since therefore Christ suffered in the flesh, arm yourselves with the same way of thinking" (1 Peter 4:1). On the one hand, we are told in the Scriptures that God is not against the Christians but for them (Romans 8:31), that they are God's children and heirs of eternal life (John 1:12–13; Galatians 3:26; Romans 8:17), that angels serve them (Hebrews 1:14), and on the other hand, Jesus tells His children: "If anyone would come after Me, let him deny himself and take up his cross and follow Me" (Mark 8:34). Jesus here refers to what is the inevitable lot of the believer in the midst of a sinful and hostile world.

What Constitutes
the Cross of the Christian?

"What Christians suffer as Christians, in living their Christian faith in this world, that properly constitutes the cross" (Francis Pieper, *Christian Dogmatics* [St. Louis: Concordia, 1953], 3:69). By the Christian cross is meant the sufferings of this present time (Romans 8:18), which we as Christians endure for Christ's and the Gospel's sake, such as bearing mockery, ridicule, shame, contempt, denying ourselves the sinful pleasures of this life, suffering persecution and, if need be, death for Jesus' sake. "All who desire to live a godly life in Christ Jesus will be persecuted" (2 Timothy 3:12). "If you are insulted for the name of Christ, you are blessed. . . . If anyone suffers as a Christian, let him not be ashamed, but let him glorify God in that name" (1 Peter 4:14, 16). "For whoever would save his life will lose it, but whoever loses his life for My sake and the gospel's will save it" (Mark 8:35). Cf. John 15:18–20; Matthew 5:11–12. The daily struggle against sin (Romans 7:14–25) and the overcoming of the flesh with its sinful affections and lusts (Galatians 5:24; Colossians 3:5) is not the least of the cross we as Christians bear. Also the contempt, the silent or open ridicule, which the wicked world heaps upon Christians is included in the Christian's cross.

For example, in order to make progress in one's profession or trade in the world, it often appears necessary to join organizations and to identify oneself with groups that do no honor to Christ but which rather dishonor Him. Without such affiliation many doors of opportunity for advancement seem closed. To deny oneself progress and advancement in the world under such conditions and circumstances is a cross that the Christian will bear. The Christian should always aim to be loyal to Christ above all things, and if it means lesser success and fewer advantages from the material standpoint, the Christian will be content with his lot.

INSEPARABLE CONNECTION
BETWEEN CHRISTIANITY AND THE CROSS

Bearing the cross is inseparably bound up with Christianity, so inseparably that he who refuses to bear the cross can no longer claim to be a Christian. "Whoever does not take his cross and follow Me is not worthy of Me" (Matthew 10:38). The cross is a necessary mark of Christian discipleship.

This does not mean, however, that the Christian may impose a cross upon himself or upon others. He must leave that to God (1 Peter 1:6; 3:17), for God alone knows which cross is beneficial, and only God gives the strength needed to bear the cross (1 Corinthians 10:13).

Every Christian has his own peculiar cross. Christians are not equally endowed; there are diversities of talents and gifts among them. So, too, Christians differ as to greatness or weakness of faith. And because God distributes our gifts, He knows in every instance just how heavy a cross each of us can carry. "God is faithful, and He will not let you be tempted beyond your ability, but with the temptation He will also provide the way of escape, that you may be able to endure it" (1 Corinthians 10:13). Whether your cross be great or small, God has fitted that cross for you.

OTHER STRINGS ON WHICH TO PLAY

One night in Vienna, Ole Bull, a Norwegian master violinist, whose early struggles would have defeated a lesser man, was playing a difficult selection from Beethoven. The E string snapped! Did Ole Bull stop? Not he. He went right on and played the difficult adagio movement with such abandon and interpretation on three strings that the audience went wild with enthusiasm. After that his fame was secure.

The greatness of the Christian life consists in being determined to go on even though something has gone wrong. There is never a time to stop and repine at our lot. The Lord denied the apostle Paul the removal of the thorn in the flesh. But Paul was content and learned to bear it patiently and without complaint.

We all have lost some of life's precious things, but we must go on and make the best arrangements for happiness and service with what we have left. And there is always enough left. There still are other strings on which to play.

Some may have lost money saved for old age; others may have lost health. Yet there are in the world many who have taken their burdened and sickened bodies and played mighty noble music upon the strings that were left. With God as our stay, and with heaven as our gracious reward, how can it be otherwise?

THE PURPOSE AND PROFIT OF THE CROSS

The cross is proof that God regards us as His children. "And if children, then heirs—heirs of God and fellow heirs with Christ, provided we suffer with Him in order that we may also be glorified with Him" (Romans 8:17). The cross belongs to the ways and means by which God leads Christians through this world into eternal life. Cf. Acts 14:22; 2 Corinthians 4:17. The cross renders us humble before God (2 Corinthians 12:7). It warns us to place our sole reliance in the grace of God (2 Corinthians 12:8–9). It thus exercises and strengthens our faith, moves us to prayer, destroys the body of sin, and in general turns our gaze heavenward to things eternal.

The purpose of the cross is to conform us to the image of the Lord in love (John 13:34), in humility (Matthew 11:29), in obedience to God (Philippians 2:5, 8), in patience under suffering (Hebrews 12:2), and in submissive prayer (Matthew 26:42). As Christ died for our sins and was raised again by the glory of the Father, even so should we be conformed to His image by being dead unto sin and by walking in newness of life (Romans 6:4).

THE RIGHT VIEW OF THE CROSS

Our flesh considers cross-bearing a heavy burden. We may even think that God has forgotten us. Scripture therefore instructs us that the cross, even though by it our sins are judged, does not manifest God's wrath against us but rather reveals God's love toward us. "For the Lord disciplines the one He loves, and chastises every son whom He receives" (Hebrews 12:6). Cf. Hebrews 12:7–10. Scripture furthermore instructs us that when we suffer because of our confession of Christ by word and deed, the cross is for us a testimony of the Holy Spirit that we belong to Christ, for we then experience the same treatment which Christ and all witnesses of Christ experienced. Scripture explicitly informs us that the sufferings of this time, by which we become like Christ, are for us a pledge of the eternal glory awaiting us (Romans 8:17). We should therefore rejoice that God uses the means of the cross to conform us ever more to Christ's image. "For to this you have been called, because Christ also suffered for you, leaving you an example, so that you might follow in His steps" (1 Peter 2:21). As Christ suffered for our sins, so we are to suffer for Christ's sake (Philippians 1:29). We are to be dead with Him that we may also live with Him; we are to suffer with Him that we may also reign with Him (2 Timothy 2:11–12).

THE AFFLICTIONS OF LIFE

Very often both Christians and unbelievers suffer the same trials, troubles, and tribulations of this life. Both may meet with an accident, both may suffer the loss of earthly goods, both may be deprived of their means of livelihood, both may be stricken with sickness, both may be the objects of calamities, disasters, and misfortunes. But there is an all-important distinction between Christians and the unbelieving children of the world in these experiences.

As for the unbelieving children of the world, all their afflictions are to be viewed as direct punishments from God for their sins. Cf. Psalm 7:11; Romans 1:18.

On the other hand, the Christian's afflictions are tokens of God's love. They are not accidental; they are not the unfortunate results of blind chance. On the contrary, our afflictions are placed upon us by God and with God's permission. God never afflicts His children without a purpose. Afflictions remind us of the greatness and terribleness of our sins and are to lead us to daily repentance. Since God by means of afflictions effects humility and repentance in His children, and since afflictions serve as a trial of their faith and develop other characteristics after the image of Christ, they, too, are part of the cross that the Christian will have to bear in this world. "We know that for those who love God all things work together for good, for those who are called according to his purpose" (Romans 8:28). "For the moment all discipline seems painful rather than pleasant, but later it yields the peaceful fruit of righteousness to those who have been trained by it" (Hebrews 12:11). The cross-bearer's future crown by the grace of God is incomparable glory.

Spiritual Refining

Abiding blessings come to us by way of affliction; for the path of the Christian in life ever remains the way of the cross. In no other way may we by the grace of God attain the realization of being with Christ in glory.

In the world of material things we note that the most precious material needs the most severe treatment to bring out its highest value and usefulness. Coarse clay needs coarse modeling before it is fit for coarse use. Wood needs only whittling and polishing. Silver needs beating but usually no more. But gold, most precious of metals, needs to go through the fiery furnace before it can make a vessel worthy of a king.

Thus in life the ultimate end cannot be attained except by a painful process. "Through many tribulations we must enter the kingdom of God" (Acts 14:22). We are not perfect children; therefore we need correction. Tribulation presents an opportunity to exercise our graces, deepens Christ's work within us, keeps us much at the throne of grace, and weans us away from the present world. It would be eternally unfortunate for us if we had no cross to bear. God's lessons are always too good to be lost and are worth all they cost to learn. With Job every child of God exclaims: "When He has tried me, I shall come out as gold" (Job 23:10).

CHAPTER 14

The Christian Church

While the word *church* is used among us in several different meanings, we are here speaking of it in its really proper sense, namely, "the Holy Christian Church, the communion of saints." It is composed of the whole number of believers in Christ. The figurative terms used in the Scriptures to describe this Church indicate that there exists an inner relation and spiritual communion between its members and God. Cf. 1 Timothy 3:15; 1 Peter 2:5, 9; Ephesians 1:22–23; 2:19, 21. To be in this intimate and personal relation with God requires that we have faith in Christ as our Savior. "For in Christ Jesus you are all sons of God, through faith" (Galatians 3:26). In the Apostles' Creed the Holy Christian Church is called "the communion of saints," because these people are declared holy before God for the sake of Jesus, whose righteousness covers their unrighteousness.

THE QUALITIES OF THE CHRISTIAN CHURCH

We speak of this Church as being invisible because no one can look into another's heart to determine whether he has faith in Christ. While "the Lord knows those who are His" (2 Timothy 2:19), He also tells us that His kingdom does not come with outward pomp and display, because it is within man (Luke 17:20–21).

There is only one Christian Church, and it includes all members in Christ the world over. Jesus speaks of "one flock, one shepherd" (John 10:16). Cf. John 11:52.

Because of the perfect righteousness of Christ that Christians accept in faith, the Christian Church is holy. "Christ loved the church and gave Himself up for her, that He might sanctify her, having cleansed her by the washing of water with the word, so that He might present the church to Himself in splendor, without spot or wrinkle or any such thing, that she might be holy and without blemish" (Ephesians 5:25–27). Christians also earnestly endeavor to lead holy lives. Cf. 1 Peter 2:5; Romans 12:1–2.

The Church is catholic, or universal, because it is gathered from every nation under the sun, wherever the Gospel is in use; for according to God's promise His Word shall not be preached in vain. Cf. Isaiah 55:10–11.

The Church is imperishable. "The gates of hell shall not prevail against it" (Matthew 16:18). Cf. Matthew 24:24; John 10:27–29; Romans 11:2–5.

Membership in this Church saves. Christ says: "I am the way, and the truth, and the life. No one comes to the Father except through Me" (John 14:6).

How Is the Church Built?

Scripture stresses that the Church is neither entirely nor in part the work of man but solely God's work and product. God "called you out of darkness into His marvelous light. Once you were not a people, but now you are God's people; once you had not received mercy, but now you have received mercy" (1 Peter 2:9–10).

The means which God employs to gather and preserve the Church is the Gospel in all its forms—the Word and the Sacraments—because only the Gospel creates and sustains saving faith. "So faith comes from hearing, and hearing through the word of Christ" (Romans 10:17). "You have been born again . . . through the living and abiding word of God. . . . The word of the Lord remains forever. And this word is the good news that was preached to you" (1 Peter 1:23, 25).

The role of man in building, spreading, and preserving the Church is merely instrumental (1 Corinthians 3:5–10), inasmuch as by men the Gospel of the kingdom is to be preached in all the world (Mark 16:15).

Neither human methods and measures nor the use of civil powers and state laws nor ecclesiastical organization and union advance the building of the Church, because the Church is a congregation of believers and is born and sustained solely by the Gospel.

THE LOCAL CONGREGATION

The local congregation is the total number of those who profess to be Christians and are united with others in a certain place. Hypocrites, who simulate the outward manifestations of believers, will be found in the visible Church, but they are not members of the true Church. Cf. Matthew 13:47–48; 22:11–12; 2 Timothy 3:5; Acts 5:1–11.

THE OFFICE OF THE KEYS

Christ has given to His Church a spiritual power, which we call "the Office of the Keys." This term indicates the opening of heaven by the forgiving of sins, and the closing of heaven by the retaining of sins. Jesus says: "As the Father has sent Me, even so I am sending you. . . . Receive the Holy Spirit. If you forgive the sins of any, they are forgiven them; if you withhold forgiveness from any, it is withheld" (John 20:21–23). "I will give you the keys of the kingdom of heaven, and whatever you bind on earth shall be bound in heaven, and whatever you loose on earth shall be loosed in heaven" (Matthew 16:19).

The Office of the Keys is the power, or authority, to preach the Word of God, to administer the Sacraments, and especially the power to forgive and to retain sins. To the Christians, who constitute the true Church, God says: "Go into all the world and proclaim the gospel to the whole creation" (Mark 16:15). "Go therefore and make disciples of all nations, baptizing them in the name of the Father and of the Son and of the Holy Spirit, teaching them to observe all that I have commanded you. And behold, I am with you always, to the end of the age" (Matthew 28:19–20). "Truly, I say to you, whatever you bind on earth shall be bound in heaven, and whatever you loose on earth shall be loosed in heaven" (Matthew 18:18).

The Word of God is the only authority in the Church, and it is the only means through which the Church can operate. The use of the Word by the Church is called "the ministry of the Word" (Acts 6:4).

To that end the Church teaches all that Christ has commanded and only what He has commanded.

Sins of penitent sinners are declared forgiven. Penitent sinners are those who feel sorry for their sins and who believe on the Lord Jesus Christ for the forgiveness of their sins. Cf. Acts 3:19. The necessary fruit of repentance is a truly Christian life. Cf. Matthew 3:8.

Sins of impenitent sinners, that is, of those who are not sorry for their sins and who do not believe on Jesus Christ, are to be retained as long as these people do not repent. The lack of repentance makes faith in Christ Jesus impossible.

How Does the Church Use the Power of the Keys?

Since each Christian belongs to "the royal priesthood" (1 Peter 2:9) and therefore possesses the authority of the Word, each Christian should exercise this authority privately; he may assure the penitent sinner of the grace of God and the forgiveness of sins through Christ, and he may declare to the impenitent that his sins are not forgiven because of his impenitence and unbelief. This may and should be done in the ordinary course of life and does not need the endorsement and support of a church organization, a congregation, or a pastor, to make it valid. Luther said: "For, though we are not all in the public office and calling [the public ministry], still every Christian should and may teach, instruct, admonish, comfort, reprove his neighbor with God's Word whenever and wherever he finds someone in need of it" (Francis Pieper, *Christian Dogmatics* [St. Louis: Concordia, 1953], 3:441). Here is a field of the Office of the Keys, which needs to be cultivated much more than it has been. The kingdom of God on earth would be the stronger for it, and the harvest of souls for heaven would be greater.

The Public Ministry

In the matter of the public exercise of the Office of the Keys, the Christian congregation calls a pastor, or public minister of the Word, who in the stead of the congregation speaks the absolution, or the declaration of the forgiveness of sins. The Office of the Public Ministry and its functions are called "public," not because they are always discharged in public, but because they are performed for the good and by the command of the public, which in this case is the congregation.

The pastoral office is a divine institution. Cf. Acts 20:28; Ephesians 4:10–12. Pastors must strictly adhere to the Word of God, preaching the pure doctrine of the Gospel and administering the Sacraments according to Christ's institution. Thereby they offer and convey to us what God Himself promises and offers in these Means of Grace, and therefore it is as valid and certain as if Christ, our dear Lord, dealt with us Himself. It has divine force and authority and is sure and reliable. We are to submit to the pastor's instructions in the Word for the Lord's sake.

Christians are invited to go to their pastor for the private confession of sins that weigh heavily on their conscience, that they might from God through the pastor receive the comforting assurance that their sins are forgiven. While this practice is nowhere commanded in Scripture, it nevertheless is a good practice, which can be of great benefit to the individual Christian. Pastors should also be sought out for counsel in spiritual matters. We may rest assured that the pastor will keep strictly to himself whatever has been confessed to him privately in confidence.

The order of the public worship service generally includes a confession of sins before God and the declaration of forgiveness, which is spoken by the pastor.

How the Congregation Is to Deal with Impenitent Sinners

Because of man's sinful state, occasions may arise within a congregation when someone becomes guilty of a public offense. When such offense is not removed, the offender must in time be excluded from the Christian congregation. Cf. 1 Corinthians 5:13. This act of exclusion is called excommunication, which means to put out or to be put out of communion. No one is ever excommunicated because of a sin that he has committed, but because of his impenitence. However, we must not act rashly in this matter of excluding people from the congregation. We should observe, where possible, the steps of admonition given in the Scriptures. The directions are given in Matthew 18:15–18. The length of time for the various steps of church discipline is not prescribed; it may vary in different cases. The object is to bring the erring one back to a right understanding of and conformance to God's Word; hence patience is to be exercised in dealing with an erring brother.

Also excommunication itself is intended not for the eternal ruin of the excommunicated or as an act of vengeance, but is intended for the salvation of his soul; he is to see the greatness of his sin and is to repent. As far as the congregation is concerned, excommunication of persistent impenitent sinners is demanded because the separation of the unworthy is required of Christians by God. Cf. 1 Corinthians 5. A Christian congregation will gladly forgive and restore to membership in the congregation an excommunicated person who repents of his sin. Cf. 2 Corinthians 2:6–10.

THE PRIVILEGE OF CHURCH MEMBERSHIP

While Christians do band themselves together in Christian congregations because it is a duty that God would have them fulfill, they do so even more because it is a privilege. The blessings of church membership are great. For a full Christian life we need the fellowship of Christians.

Members meet in a local Christian congregation to build themselves up in the doctrine of the apostles and the prophets. They are taught in God's Word, reminded of God's promises and of their own duties to God and man, corrected in their life, warned of the dangers in this world, and comforted in their trials. But they join a Christian congregation also because of the service they might give in such an association. While it is true that most of the Christian service is done in other life relationships, independent of the congregation (family, community, business), there still remain some things that can best be done jointly. The local Christian congregation affords us the opportunity to participate in larger, even worldwide projects.

The chief purpose of church membership is to aid us on the way to heaven and to give us the opportunity to help others on the same way. With such high objectives and such noble projects, membership in a local Christian congregation is not begged and fawningly solicited but is presented as an honor and a privilege, which it truly is.

CHAPTER 15

The Sacraments

God has given His children certain ordinances, which they are to observe in the Church. These we call the sacraments.

The word *sacrament* is not a biblical term. It is derived from a word meaning "to consecrate." Originally a sacrament signified an oath or a solemn engagement, as the military oath of a Roman soldier, by which he renounced allegiance to everyone else and swore loyalty to the Roman emperor. Because in the Early Church the adult Christians at their Baptism renounced all idols and swore allegiance to Christ, which vow really was their "sacramentum," the term was eventually applied to Baptism itself. Later it was applied also to the Lord's Supper.

The Meaning of Sacrament

Since there are currently several meanings attached to the word *sacrament*, it is well to state here what we understand by it and how we use the term. By a sacrament we mean a sacred act of God, instituted by God Himself, carried out by the Church, in which there are certain visible means connected with the use of God's Word, by which God offers, gives, and seals to us the forgiveness of sins that Christ has earned for us. The sacraments offer the same grace of God and the same blessings that are offered in the Gospel. Faith in Christ as the Savior is required to obtain these blessings. According to our definition of a sacrament there are two: the Sacrament of Holy Baptism and the Sacrament of the Altar.

The Sacrament of Holy Baptism

Christ instituted Baptism when He said: "Go therefore and make disciples of all nations, baptizing them in the name of the Father and of the Son and of the Holy Spirit" (Matthew 28:19). While the right and duty to baptize is given to the whole Church, Baptism ordinarily is administered by the pastor of a Christian congregation.

Visible Means

The external element, or the visible means, in Baptism is water, as we see from the word *baptize*, which means "to apply water, to wash." The mode of applying water in Baptism is not indicated in the Scriptures, neither does it depend on the amount of water used or where it is applied. It may be applied by pouring, washing, sprinkling, or immersing.

In Baptism water is applied "in the name of the Father and of the Son and of the Holy Spirit" (Matthew 28:19), which means that we enter into a covenant relation with God and are partakers of all the blessings of His grace. In Baptism we "put on Christ" (Galatians 3:27).

Baptize All Nations

According to the Scriptures "all nations" are to be baptized; this includes men, women, and children. Adults are instructed first and then baptized. Cf. Acts 2:41; 8:26–40; 10:47–48. In their case Baptism establishes and makes firm the grace of God and strengthens them in their faith. Little children are baptized without previous instruction. They are by Baptism born into the Christian Church. As they reach the age of reason and understanding, they are to be taught the Word of God.

Wash Away Our Sins

In Holy Baptism God washes away our sins. We are baptized "for the forgiveness of sins" (Acts 2:38). Cf. Mark 16:16; Acts 22:16; Ephesians 5:26. Baptism delivers us from eternal death (Romans 6:3). It gives us eternal salvation. "Baptism . . . now saves you" (1 Peter 3:21).

We accept the gifts of Holy Baptism by faith in the promises of God's Word. The mere application of water in the name of the Father and of the Son and of the Holy Spirit does not grant the baptized the blessings of Baptism. Faith, which trusts the Word of God, is necessary. The one who believes the promise of God's Word receives what God offers in Baptism. "Whoever believes and is baptized will be saved, but whoever does not believe will be condemned" (Mark 16:16). Cf. Galatians 3:26–27.

Remember Baptism Daily

While Baptism is administered only once in a person's life, it is designed to be of meaning every day of our life, and we should use it profitably all our days. Many forget their Baptism and thus deprive themselves of much comfort and strengthening. The daily remembrance of our Baptism should strengthen us in the faith that in Christ all our sins are forgiven and that we are the children of God. "For in Christ Jesus you are all sons of God, through faith. For as many of you as were baptized into Christ have put on Christ" (Galatians 3:26–27). The remembrance of our Baptism should urge us to suppress the old Adam by crucifying our evil affections and lusts (Ephesians 4:22; Galatians 5:24), and should urge us to live righteous and holy lives (2 Corinthians 5:17; Ephesians 4:24; Romans 6:4). Thus Baptism can and should have a powerful meaning to us all the days of our life.

THE SACRAMENT OF THE ALTAR

This sacrament, also known as Holy Communion and the Lord's Supper, was instituted by Christ on the evening before He died on Calvary. The summarized account of the institution as recorded in Matthew 26:26–28; Mark 14:22–24; Luke 22:19–20; 1 Corinthians 11:23–25, is as follows: "Our Lord Jesus Christ, the same night in which He was betrayed, took bread; and when He had given thanks, He broke it and gave it to His disciples, saying, 'Take, eat; this is My body, which is given for you. This do in remembrance of Me.' In the same way also He took the cup after supper, and when He had given thanks, He gave it to them, saying, 'Drink of it all of you; this cup is the new testament in My blood, which is shed for you for the remission of sin. This do, as often as you drink it, in remembrance of Me.' " Accordingly Dr. Martin Luther describes the Sacrament of the Altar in this way: "It is the true body and blood of our Lord Jesus Christ under the bread and wine, instituted by Christ Himself for us Christians to eat and to drink" (Small Catechism).

Visible Means

The visible external means, which Jesus used, were unleavened bread and grape wine; hence we also use these means. Together with the bread Christ gives us His true body, and together with the wine Christ gives us His true blood. We cannot comprehend how this can be, but we believe it because Christ says it is so. Elsewhere the Scriptures speak of a communion of the wine and the blood and a communion of the bread and the body (1 Corinthians 10:16), which plainly indicates that four things are truly and really present, distributed, and received by all communicants. To say that the bread signifies or represents or symbolizes the body, and the wine the blood, is contrary to the Scriptures. It is just as wrong to say that the bread and the wine are changed into the body and blood of Christ. Cf. 1 Corinthians 11:26–28. Furthermore, the presence of Christ's body and blood in this sacrament does not indicate worship of the same. Neither are we to regard the Lord's Supper as an additional or supplementary sacrifice, though unbloody, for the sins of the living and of the dead. Christ by His offering on the cross "has perfected for all time those who are being sanctified" (Hebrews 10:14). The Lord's Supper is a means through which the forgiveness of sins is assured to us.

All communicants are to participate in the eating and the drinking, for this is a necessary part in the celebration of the Lord's Supper. Cf. 1 Corinthians 11:20–27.

In Remembrance of Christ

Christ says regarding this sacrament: "This do in remembrance of Me." We should especially remember three things: (1) We should in sorrow remember that our sins made a Savior and His sacrifice on the cross necessary; (2) we should in true faith remember that Jesus is the one and only Savior, who fully atoned for our sins before God; (3) we should in gratitude remember that we are to lead righteous lives. By partaking of the Lord's Supper we "show His death" (1 Corinthians 11:26), which means that we confess our faith in the redemptive death of our Lord.

Do Often

Christians will frequently receive the Lord's Supper. It is our Lord's will that we go often, as the words of institution indicate. Cf. 1 Corinthians 11:26. We attend frequently also because we desire the assurance of the forgiveness of our sins and of the bestowal of God's grace. When we realize how evil the promptings of our heart are, how inviting to evil the world is, and how determined the devil is to assault us, we are incited to frequent communing in order to strengthen and gird ourselves for a godly life in an ungodly world.

In the Lord's Supper Christ makes the assurance of forgiveness certain. The Lord's Supper is a pledge and guarantee, for Christ comes to each communicant and says: "My body is given for you and My blood is shed for you for the forgiveness of your sins." We are assured, as we can be in no other way, that, what Christ did, He did for us as individuals. To be worthy guests at the Lord's Table requires that we believe in Christ as our personal Savior from sin.

Self-Examination for a Worthy Communion

In order to be worthy communicants, we are advised by the Lord through the apostle Paul to make a careful preparation before we commune. "Let a person examine himself, then, and so eat of the bread and drink of the cup" (1 Corinthians 11:28). We should examine ourselves to see (1) whether we truly repent of our sins, (2) whether we believe in Jesus Christ as our Savior, and (3) whether we have the good and earnest purpose with the aid of the Holy Spirit to live a more Christlike life in the future. The unwillingness or inability to examine oneself according to God's Word disqualifies a person to commune. This includes the ungodly and impenitent, those who have given offense and failed to remove it, those who bear an ill will toward anyone, and those who have not been indoctrinated sufficiently to make a self-examination. It also includes those of a different faith, for the Lord's Supper is also a testimony to the oneness of faith. Cf. Romans 16:17; 1 Corinthians 10:16–21.

We Christians will come to the Lord's Supper as poor sinners who know that we cannot save ourselves. We will come confessing that we have sinned in thought, word, and deed and that we deserve God's eternal punishment. "The sacrifices of God are a broken spirit; a broken and contrite heart, O God, You will not despise" (Psalm 51:17). "God, be merciful to me, a sinner" (Luke 18:13) is our prayer.

Above all else we will come as believers in Christ Jesus. We cannot approach God in any acceptable capacity unless we come in the name of Jesus. Our plea of acceptance is based wholly on Christ and on His merits. We come believing that His shed blood is our one hope of salvation. We also believe that Jesus is able to redeem the promise He makes in this sacrament.

Blessings and Responsibility

With the great blessings, which are given us in the Lord's Supper, are coupled also grave responsibilities, which we cheerfully assume. We come with the intention to live more Christlike in the future. This means we shall strive to forsake sin and follow God's way of life. Repentance and faith are sincere only when they are coupled with an earnest desire for the improvement of life.

Such a self-examination is of utmost importance for the beneficial partaking of the Lord's Supper, and he who makes it can rest assured that Jesus tells him at the Communion table: "Your sins are forgiven you."

CHAPTER 16

Death and the Life Hereafter

Christians have the hope of a future inheritance in heaven; they know there is a life eternal. The apostle Paul says: "If in Christ we have hope in this life only, we are of all people most to be pitied" (1 Corinthians 15:19). To accept the teachings of Christianity and to champion the Christian cause without possessing a hope for the future is vain and a foolish delusion. Christianity is founded on the life, death, and resurrection of Christ; this assures our eternal well-being. "For God so loved the world, that He gave His only Son, that whoever believes in Him should not perish but have eternal life" (John 3:16). There is a life to come.

Natural man lacks positive evidence about eternal life. Yet he senses that man's conscious existence and personal identity continue beyond the life on this earth. Hence almost every religion speaks of a life beyond the grave. If life ended at the grave, this would seem an irrational world.

We have the testimony of the inspired writers of the Scriptures that there is a life hereafter. When Jesus speaks of the God of Abraham, of Isaac, and of Jacob, who had departed this world centuries before, He calls Him a God of the living. Cf. Luke 20:38; Exodus 3:6. Accordingly the souls of the righteous of all times are alive. This is true of all believers of all times. And from 1 Peter 3:18–19 we learn that the souls of the people who during their life here on earth had been disobedient also are existing after leaving this world; they are called "the spirits in prison." Scores of Bible passages could be cited to show that Jesus teaches a life hereafter, or a life in the world to come. Innumerable times He speaks of His children as heirs of eternal life, and of the ungodly as those who are on the way to everlasting damnation.

The parable of the rich man and Lazarus (Luke 16:19–31) teaches that there is a life hereafter for both the evil and the good. The story of the final judgment (Matthew 25:31–46) teaches a life hereafter for all people.

DEATH

To enter life hereafter, we pass through death. Death is the cessation of natural life. It is not a total destruction or the annihilation of man but is the loss of physical life on this earth, which is caused by the separation of body and soul. Cf. 2 Peter 1:13–14. We read of the rich man in Luke 12:20 that his soul was required of him that night; his soul was to depart from his body; he was to die. When Christ died, He "yielded up His spirit" (Matthew 27:50); His dead body remained on the cross while His soul entered paradise. Death is described in Ecclesiastes 12:7 in this manner: "The dust [body] returns to the earth as it was, and the spirit [soul] returns to God who gave it" Accordingly, temporal death is the separation of body and soul in an individual person.

THE CAUSE OF DEATH

Man is not subject to death according to the order of creation, since God did not create Adam and Eve to die. Man therefore has a natural horror of death. Death is a part of God's threat as a punishment of sin (Genesis 2:17; 3:19). Death entered into the world by sin (Romans 5:12). "The wages of sin is death" (Romans 6:23). Cf. James 1:15.

Because of sin in the life of all mankind we live and die by the will of God. "You return man to dust" (Psalm 90:3). God terminates the lives of men in various ways, by many means, and at different ages. However, whatever may be the physical cause of death, all men die of their own sins (Psalm 90:7–9).

Because sin is universal among men, so also is death. Man, who was created to live, is now born to die; his way through life leads to the grave. "It is appointed for man to die once" (Hebrews 9:27). "Death spread to all men because all sinned" (Romans 5:12). Those who are still living at the coming of Christ to judgment will not die. Cf. 1 Corinthians 15:51.

Death Does Not End Man's Existence

Death does not terminate man's existence. At death body and soul separate. The material body decays and returns to the ground, dust to dust (Genesis 3:19; Ecclesiastes 3:20); in this state it continues until the Last Day.

The disembodied soul, an immaterial, spiritual creation of God, does not dissolve and vanish into the air; nor is it absorbed into the Being of God. As a created spirit, endowed with immortality by God, the soul continues to exist after death as a distinct personal entity. To the thief on the cross Jesus said: "Today you will be with Me in Paradise" (Luke 23:43), even though that man's body was buried somewhere on the day he died. While the bodies of the rich man and of Lazarus in the parable (Luke 16:22–23) were buried after they died, their souls continued to exist. Paul the apostle states that he desired to be with Christ (Philippians 1:23), referring to his departure from this world in death. This separate existence of the soul continues until it is reunited with its body on the Last Day (1 Kings 17:22; John 5:28–29; 11:24). Death does not end the existence of man.

Where Are the Souls of the Dead?

Jesus said to the penitent thief that in the moment of death his soul was to enter paradise. In his hour of death Stephen said: "Lord Jesus, receive my spirit [soul]" (Acts 7:59). Whoever dies in the Lord, that is, whoever dies a Christian, is blessed "from now on" (Revelation 14:13). The apostle Paul desired to "be with Christ," and he added that this would be "far better" for him than to continue in the flesh (Philippians 1:23–24). In 2 Corinthians 5:8, the apostle states: "We are of good courage, and we would rather be away from the body and at home with the Lord"; this means that the disembodied souls of the Christians rest with Jesus. For this reason we pray that finally, when our last hour has come, God would "grant us a blessed end and graciously take us from this valley of sorrows to Himself in heaven."

The souls of the unbelievers are "in prison" (1 Peter 3:19–20). Judas, after he took his own life, went to "his place" (Acts 1:25). The parable of the rich man and Lazarus teaches that the condition of the wicked after death is one of torment (Luke 16:23).

The departed souls remain in heaven or in hell until the Day of Judgment, when they shall be reunited with their bodies. Then the believers shall in their flesh see God (Job 19:26), while the unbelievers shall according to body and soul be consigned to eternal torment (Matthew 10:28).

SOME FALSE NOTIONS DISPELLED

The souls of the departed do not return to this earth to communicate with the living. The dead are ignorant of us (Isaiah 63:16) and will not be sent even on a mission of mercy to warn a sinner (Luke 16: 27–29).

There is no transmigration of souls, as taught by some who believe that at death the soul passes into another body for the purpose of purification, and then finally returns to God. This process, according to these advocates, may be repeated a number of times. The Scriptures know of no transmigration of souls.

There is, according to the Scriptures, no purgatory, in which the full and final salvation of the soul is supposed to be accomplished by its own suffering and by the prayers and alms offered in its behalf by the living people on earth. The doctrine of purgatory is false, for it denies the sufficiency of the merits of Christ and of the free and full remission of sins through faith in Christ. There are only two places into which the departed soul enters. Cf. Matthew 7:13–14.

WHEN IS THE ETERNAL DESTINY
OF MAN DECIDED?

The eternal destiny of man is decided the moment he dies. At that time the opportunity to accept God's grace comes to an end. He that believes shall be saved, and he that believes not shall be damned (Mark 16:16). After death there is no opportunity for improving one's condition, no second chance, no further offer of grace and forgiveness. "When the wicked dies, his hope will perish, and the expectation of wealth perishes too" (Proverbs 11:7). While we live on earth it "is the favorable time . . . is the day of salvation" (2 Corinthians 6:2). "It is appointed for man to die once, and after that comes judgment" (Hebrews 9:27). Cf. John 3:36; 5:24; Revelation 2:10; 14:13.

LIFE HEREAFTER AND THE TRANSITORY NATURE OF THIS WORLD

Jesus was always pointing to the life hereafter, and in doing so He emphasized the transitory nature of this world in which we live. Jesus says in the Scriptures: "Do not lay up for yourselves treasures on earth, where moth and rust destroy and where thieves break in and steal, but lay up for yourselves treasures in heaven, where neither moth nor rust destroys and where thieves do not break in and steal" (Matthew 6:19–20). "Heaven and earth will pass away" (Luke 21:33). "The present form of this world is passing away" (1 Corinthians 7:31). Christ speaks of the signs of His coming to judgment and of the end of the world in Matthew 24.

We do not know when the end of the world will come, but we know from the Scriptures that it will coincide with the day of Christ's coming to judgment. Cf. 2 Peter 3:4, 10; Matthew 24:3.

The Scriptures have not spoken plainly in the matter of the destruction of the world. It may be either a destruction by annihilation, or it may be a destruction by renovation. Some think that the entire fabric and substance of heaven and earth will be annihilated and that God will create a new heaven and a new earth. Others hold that the form, the present appearance, of this world will be destroyed, but that its fundamental substance will not be destroyed; this substance will be used by God to fashion a new heaven and a new earth. It is not important for us to know how this world will be destroyed. Cf. Luke 21:33; Hebrews 1:10–12; Matthew 24:3; Isaiah 65:17; 1 Corinthians 7:31; 2 Peter 3:11–13.

THE RESURRECTION OF THE BODY

Existence according to body and soul in the life to come necessitates the resurrection of the body. The fact of the resurrection of the body can be established only from the Scriptures, which speak very definitely on this subject.

Faith in Christ carries with it the hope of a resurrection. Cf. John 11:25–26. The resurrection of Jesus Christ from the dead on Easter Day proves that there is a resurrection of the body. Cf. 1 Corinthians 15:12–20.

On the basis of Scripture every Christian confesses: "I believe the resurrection of the dead." "There will be a resurrection of both the just and the unjust" (Acts 24:15). Cf. John 5:28–29. Christ's call to repentance in this world is being rejected by many, but His call to arise on the Day of Judgment will be obeyed by all. Cf. Revelation 20:12–13. In speaking only of Christians, Jesus says: "I will raise him up on the last day" (John 6:40). Cf. 1 Thessalonians 4:16. In 1 Corinthians 15, Paul infers that because of Christ's resurrection our resurrection becomes a certainty and that this resurrection will take place when Christ comes to judge the world.

When Christ will call the dead from their graves, the people still living on earth will have their bodies changed by transformation; they will not die. Cf. 1 Corinthians 15:51–52.

THE IDENTITY OF PERSON WILL BE PRESERVED

The same body that died and decayed will be restored, and the same soul that departed from the body in death will again make this body its dwelling place. The identity of person will be fully preserved in the resurrection. Job says: "In my flesh I shall see God . . . and my eyes shall behold, and not another" (Job 19:26–27). Moses and Elijah on the Mount of Transfiguration were the same persons as the Moses and Elijah we read about in the Old Testament (Matthew 17:2–4). The resurrected Christ was the identical person that died on the cross (Luke 24:39). The identity of person is taught in Luke 16:19–31. Nothing can hinder God from bringing back to each soul its own body.

THE CONDITION OF THE BODY
IN THE HEREAFTER

The resurrected body will be endowed with new attributes and qualities, adapted to the nature and the circumstances then existing. Because it will henceforth be inseparably united with the immortal soul, the body will likewise be immortal and incorruptible. Nor will it be subject to those physical laws and conditions by which it was controlled in this earthly life, for the former things will have passed away. However, not all bodies will have the same manner of living. The wicked will be condemned to everlasting torment. The righteous will be eternally saved and will dwell in the presence of God.

THE FINAL JUDGMENT

The final judgment ushers in life hereafter for the reunited body and soul of man. The idea of some future judgment and retribution is not peculiar to the Christian religion. In some forms we find it also in many pagan religions. Cf. Romans 1:32; 2:15. Reliable information concerning the final judgment we can get only from the Scriptures.

Date Unknown to Man

On the Last Day Christ will appear (Matthew 25:31). The Last Day will come suddenly and unexpectedly, "like a thief" (2 Peter 3:10), and "as the lightning comes from the east and shines as far as the west, so will be the coming of the Son of Man" (Matthew 24:27). Signs that indicate its near approach are recorded in Matthew 24; Luke 21; 2 Thessalonians 2.

Christ will raise the dead (John 5:28–29) and will judge the world in righteousness (Acts 17:31; 2 Timothy 4:1); everyone will receive full justice.

The place of the final judgment has not been revealed. The Son of Man shall come in the clouds of heaven and shall send forth His angels to gather the elect (Matthew 24:30–31) and all nations before Him (Matthew 25:31–32). Then the believers still living at that time and the resurrected believers shall be caught up in the clouds and shall meet the Lord in the air (1 Thessalonians 4:16–17).

Christ Will Be the Judge

Christ Jesus will be the Judge. The same Jesus who in the fullness of time assumed the human nature, who redeemed us by His life and death, who on the third day after His death arose from the dead, will judge all mankind. Jesus "is the one appointed by God to be judge of the living and the dead" (Acts 10:42). God has given Jesus "authority to execute judgment, because He is the Son of Man" (John 5:27). "When the Son of Man comes in His glory, and all the angels with Him, then He will sit on His glorious throne. Before Him will be gathered all the nations, and He will separate people one from another as a shepherd separates the sheep from the goats. And He will place the sheep on His right, but the goats on the left" (Matthew 25:31–33). All must appear before the judgment seat of Christ to be judged. No one will be overlooked; no one can escape. Also the fallen angels will receive their final sentence (2 Peter 2:4; Matthew 8:29).

Believers in Christ will participate in the judgment of the world, according to 1 Corinthians 6:2–3. So intimate and perfect is the union of the believers with Christ, their Head, that, when the Head appears in the glory of the judgment, the believers also will take part in this judicial function.

The Rule of Judgment

The standard and rule of judgment are the works of men. "So that each one may receive what is due for what he has done in the body, whether good or evil" (2 Corinthians 5:10). The righteous are judged only according to their good works because these works are the proof of their faith in Christ; the evil works of believers are not even brought to light because they have been forgiven (Micah 7:19). The unrighteous are judged on the basis of their works, which reveal their lack of faith in Christ and His Gospel. Cf. Matthew 25:34–46. So it resolves itself into this, that the presence or absence of faith in the Gospel is the determining factor. If Christ were to judge by the Law, no man would be saved. "If You, O Lord, should mark iniquities, O Lord, who could stand?" (Psalm 130:3). Christ will judge according to man's reaction to the Gospel. "The word that I have spoken will judge him on the last day" (John 12:48); from the preceding verse we must infer that "the Word" is the Gospel, which men receive in faith or reject in unbelief. Regarding this matter Paul writes: "On that day when, according to my gospel, God judges the secrets of men by Christ Jesus" (Romans 2:16). Christ will judge the individual according to his personal attitude toward this Gospel, whether he accepted it in faith or rejected it in unbelief. Cf. Mark 16:16; John 3:18; 5:24; 2 Thessalonians 1:7–10.

Because they believe the Gospel of salvation through Christ, the believers will not be condemned, but will stand justified before God. "The judgment is abolished; it concerns the believer as little as it does the angels," says Dr. Martin Luther (Francis Pieper, *Christian Dogmatics* [St. Louis: Concordia, 1953], 3:541). Cf. John 3:16–18; 5:24. Their works will be mentioned (Matthew 25:35–40), not as a saving factor, but as the public evidence of that faith whereby they were the children of God. Good works are the visible fruit of an invisible faith.

With the unbelievers the curse of the Law will take its course, because they rejected the grace of God in Christ Jesus, offered freely in the Gospel. The wrath of God, which they provoked by their sins, abides on them (Ephesians 5:5–6). Because they did not believe in Christ for the forgiveness of their sins, they must die in their sins. "For unless you believe that I am He you will die in your sins" (John 8:24).

Eternal Damnation

For the unbelievers, who refuse salvation through Christ, the life hereafter will be one of everlasting punishment. Hell and damnation are not a fiction but a stern and dreadful reality. In Matthew 18:8–9, Christ speaks of the everlasting hellfire. The apostle Paul speaks of a "punishment of eternal destruction, away from the presence of the Lord" (2 Thessalonians 1:9). When, therefore, on the Last Day the sentence of condemnation, "Depart from Me, you cursed, into the eternal fire prepared for the devil and his angels," is passed, it will be carried out immediately, for the Scriptures read: "And these will go into eternal punishment" (Matthew 25:41, 46).

Meaning of Damnation

To be damned in hell means to be forever rejected and banished from the blissful presence of God. The damned shall be cast into outer darkness, where there is weeping and gnashing of teeth (Matthew 8:12); the outer darkness represents hell, contrasted with the banquet hall, which is brightly illuminated and which represents heaven. Cf. Matthew 22:11–13. The suffering of the lost is intensified by the fact that they will be aware of the saints in heaven (Luke 13:28). They are tormented in body and soul and are utterly forsaken of God (Matthew 10:28; Luke 16:23–24). For the torment of hell there is no relief; from hell there is no escape; to the sufferings of hell there is no end, for it is an everlasting punishment (Matthew 25:46) and an everlasting destruction (2 Thessalonians 1:9) in an unquenchable fire, where their misery never ends (Mark 9:43–48). In hell there is no hope. The condemned shall be objects of contempt (Daniel 12:2) and an abhorring to all flesh (Isaiah 66:24).

Degrees of Punishment

While the punishment for all in hell will be continuous and everlasting, there will be varying degrees of punishment. The general rule laid down in Luke 12:47–48 applies also to the lost in hell, for according to Matthew 11:16–24 those who rejected the Gospel preached to them will fare worse in judgment than those who never heard it. Cf. Matthew 10:14–15. Judgment will be according to privilege. The greater the grace, the greater the responsibility. On the Day of Judgment all these things will be taken into account and sentence rendered accordingly.

The place of hell cannot be fixed geographically; but we know that God has assigned a place where the condemned will suffer everlasting punishment. This is evident from the many statements of Christ on the subject of eternal damnation.

The purpose of Scripture in telling us of hell and damnation is to warn us to flee from the wrath to come (Matthew 3:7, 12) and to urge us to pray that we may be accounted worthy to escape all those things and to stand before the Son of Man (Luke 21:36).

ETERNAL SALVATION

By the grace of God it is possible for us to stand before the Son of Man, our Lord Jesus Christ, and to inherit eternal salvation. This fact is clearly taught in the Scriptures. "For God so loved the world, that He gave His only Son, that whoever believes in Him should not perish but have eternal life" (John 3:16). Eternal life is a gift of God (Romans 6:23), which Christ gives to His children (John 10:28). Unto them He will say on the Day of Judgment: "Come, you who are blessed by My Father, inherit the kingdom prepared for you from the foundation of the world" (Matthew 25:34); and these shall go into eternal life (25:46).

Meaning of Salvation

Eternal salvation is the state of bliss that is due to an existence of perfect joy in the presence of God, undisturbed and unmolested by any influence of evil. To convey to us a faint idea of the surpassing splendor and glory and joy of heaven, the Bible employs terms and illustrations drawn from our earthly life. These terms must be taken figuratively, for they are intended to set forth the beauty of that heavenly place. Thus the Bible speaks of heaven as a marriage (Matthew 25:10; Revelation 19:9), as a banquet, as a sitting upon thrones (Luke 22:30), as a house with many mansions (John 14:2). Also in figurative language the Bible gives a detailed description of the heavenly Jerusalem, that city fair and high (Revelation 21:10–27); things most esteemed on earth are used in this picture to represent things in heaven, in order to give us the highest and best ideas of them.

Different External Conditions

We do know that external conditions in the world to come will be very different from present-day conditions. Certain institutions, essential and fundamental to life on the present earth, will not exist in heaven. There will be no matrimony (Matthew 22:30), no separate families, races, and nationalities. There will be no civil government, no earthly vocations to alleviate suffering and to provide the necessities of life (Revelation 7:14–17). There will be no Christian church work or mission endeavors as we know them on this earth. The wicked will not live among the saints to vex and to harass them, for the tares will be separated from the wheat (Matthew 13:30). Cf. Revelation 22:15. We shall live in the company of just men made perfect.

Spiritual Bodies

The condition of our bodies will be different in heaven. We ourselves shall be the same persons we now are, but we shall be changed (1 Corinthians 15:52). We shall have spiritual bodies, not subject to the same needs and laws which now govern us. We shall be as the angels of God (Matthew 22:30), who neither marry nor are given in marriage. We shall have incorruptible bodies, free from all traces and consequences of sin. We shall have strong bodies, free from all frailties, weaknesses, defects, deformities, and infirmities. We shall have immortal bodies, which shall never die. We shall have glorious bodies, clothed with beauty, perfection, honor and glory (1 Corinthians 15:43). God "will transform our lowly body to be like His [Christ's] glorious body" (Philippians 3:21). Believers "will shine like the sun in the kingdom of their Father" (Matthew 13:43).

Restoration of the Image of God

As for the souls, the image of God will be fully restored. "Beloved, we are God's children now, and what we will be has not yet appeared; but we know that when He appears we shall be like Him, because we shall see Him as He is" (1 John 3:2). In the world to come we shall behold God's likeness (Psalm 17:15). Since the image of God consists in the blissful knowledge of God and in righteousness and true holiness, therefore we shall then "know fully, even as [we] have been fully known" (1 Corinthians 13:12). We shall fully know God, His will, and His ways; we shall understand what now is still dark to us. All our questions both with respect to certain mysteries and to happenings in our personal life on earth will be fully answered (1 Corinthians 13:9–12). There will be no old Adam in us, no temptation around us, no sin, no sorrow, no grief (Revelation 21:4). There will be perfect righteousness and holiness. Among the residents of heaven there will be complete harmony with the will of God. There will be full satisfaction, perfect contentment, absolute security. No one shall be able to take the joys and pleasures of heaven from us. Jesus promises us "eternal life" (John 3:16, 36). In Christ's presence "are pleasures forevermore" (Psalm 16:11). The cause and source of all this heavenly bliss is God, in whose presence we shall live and whom we shall see as He is (1 John 3:2).

Degrees of Glory

The Scriptures indicate that while all saints will enjoy the same heavenly bliss, there will be degrees of glory. "Behold, I am coming soon," says Christ, "bringing My recompense with Me, to repay each one for what he has done" (Revelation 22:12). Not one of the good works will be forgotten. This gracious reward will be given to those who in their life on earth showed their faith in consecrated service to the Lord (Luke 19:12–19; Daniel 12:3), in many good works done to their fellow men (Galatians 6:8–9), and in suffering for the Lord's sake (Matthew 5:11–12). Cf. 1 Corinthians 3:11–15. "Whoever sows sparingly will also reap sparingly, and whoever sows bountifully will also reap bountifully" (2 Corinthians 9:6). Thus there shall be degrees of glory in the kingdom of glory. All saints, regardless of their degree of glory, will have in their eternal possession the heavenly salvation that Christ has earned for them. In that respect all saints will be alike. However, special rewards of grace in the form of increased glory will be given by God to us for the good works that we as sanctified children of God do on earth. If our fruits of faith during this earthly life are many, great will be the degree of glory. If our fruits of faith are few, less will be the degree of glory. The greater glory of one shall not be a cause of envy, but a source of joy, to the fellow saints.

The location of the new heaven and the new earth cannot be fixed and determined. We may say that heaven is wherever God reveals Himself to us in His uncovered glory and where we shall see Him face to face. Just where this will be need not concern us. Let us rather labor that we, too, may enter into the rest which remains for the people of God (Hebrews 4:9–11).

Cheerfully, Optimistically We Look Heavenward

The doctrine of eternal salvation has an important bearing on our present life, though its full realization pertains to the life hereafter. When we here live in the light of the life to come, we shall have a God-pleasing meaning for our sojourn on earth. We shall in this time of grace repent of our sins and believe in Christ Jesus for our salvation. We shall be careful to remain in the faith unto the end. "But the one who endures to the end will be saved" (Matthew 24:13). We shall not follow the sinful ideas and ways of this world but will walk in the ways of God (Romans 12:2). We shall set our affection on things above (Colossians 3:2). The expectation of heaven will incite us to greater efforts in holiness of life (2 Peter 3:13–14) and to laying up treasures for ourselves in heaven (Matthew 6:20). In particular we shall be interested and constantly active in bringing Christ to all people by spreading His Gospel among the lost children of men (Mark 16:15). The thought of heaven will keep us cheerful and optimistic, and no cross or affliction will discourage us, for we know, when we are tried, that in time we shall "receive the crown of life, which God has promised to those who love Him" (James 1:12). The prospect of eternal salvation fills our hearts with courage and joy and with a sustaining hope in life and death. Like the apostle Paul we look forward to the day when the Judge, our Savior Jesus Christ, will give us a crown of righteousness (2 Timothy 4:8).

CHAPTER 17

My Resolve

In the light of what the Word of God has taught me, I resolve to be a witness unto Christ, even as my Lord desires me to be. The Scriptures have taught me the basis of true joy and confident living. In Christ I know security, affection, recognition, and purposeful living. So that others, too, may learn to know the love of God in Christ Jesus, become witnesses unto Him, and in the world to come dwell with God in heaven, I resolve the following:

"I shall bear witness to the fact that I have security in Christ, for 'the LORD is my Shepherd, I shall not want' (Psalm 23:1);

"I shall bear witness to the fact that I live in the knowledge of God's love, for 'God shows His love for us in that while we were still sinners, Christ died for us' (Romans 5:8);

"I shall bear witness to the fact that God recognizes me and all mankind and that all are important in His sight, as is evident from His loving care and His redeeming work through Christ;

"I shall bear witness to the fact that nothing so enlarges life and gives purpose and zest in a truly satisfying manner as does faith in God and in His promises, 'for God, who said, "Let light shine out of darkness," has shone in our hearts to give the light of the knowledge of the glory of God in the face of Jesus Christ' (2 Corinthians 4:6).

"So help me, God."

STUDY QUESTIONS (Numbers after questions refer to pages)

AFFLICTION

1. What constitutes affliction? 151

2. Why do unbelievers suffer affliction? 151

3. Why do Christians suffer affliction? 152

4. Why is affliction a part of the Christian's cross? 152

AGNOSTICS

1. What is an agnostic? 11

2. In what sense are agnostics religious? 11

ANGELS

1. Who are the angels? 40

2. What is the ministry of the good angels? 41

3. When do we enjoy the ministry of the good angels? 41

4. How did some angels become evil? 41

5. How did an evil angel bring sin into the world? 47–48

6. What do evil angels seek to do with human beings? 41

7. What is the final fate of the evil angels? 174

ATHEISTS

1. What is an atheist? 11

2. In what sense are atheists religious? 11

3. What does the Bible call atheists? 23

BAPTISM

1. What is Baptism? 161–62

2. What external means is used in Baptism? 162

3. How may water be applied in Baptism? 162

4. What formula is to be used in Baptism? 162

CHRIST

1. Which two natures are found in Christ and when did they originate? 92

2. What does the Bible say about Christ's divine nature? 94

3. What does the Bible say about Christ's human nature? 93, 95

4. How are the two natures united in Christ? 95

5. What particular work did Christ perform for humanity? 83–97

6. Why did Christ have to be man to save us? 93, 95–98

7. Why did Christ have to be God to save us? 94

8. What do the Scriptures mean by the humiliation of Christ? 95–97

9. What do the Scriptures teach regarding the conception of Christ? 97

10. What do the Scriptures teach regarding the birth of Christ? 98

11. What do the Scriptures teach regarding Christ's suffering and death? 98

12. What do the Scriptures teach regarding the burial of Christ? 99

13. What do the Scriptures mean by the exaltation of Christ? 99–100

14. What do the Scriptures teach regarding Christ's descent into hell? 100

15. What do the Scriptures teach regarding Christ's resurrection from the dead? 101–02

16. What do the Scriptures teach regarding Christ's ascension into heaven? 102

17. What do the Scriptures teach regarding Christ's session at God's right hand? 103

18. What do the Scriptures teach regarding Christ's coming to judgment? 103, 174

19. What is meant by the prophetic office of Christ? 104

20. What is meant by the priestly office of Christ? 105

21. What is meant by the kingly office of Christ? 106

CHRISTIANITY

1. Why is Christianity the only true and right religion? 14
2. What is the basis of the Christian religion? 13–14, 110
3. What is the only source book of the Christian religion? 15–17
4. How do we become Christians? 109–10
5. What are the prospects for the Christians? 177

CHURCH

1. What is the basic meaning of the word "church"? 153
2. What is the visible Church? 155
3. What are the qualities of the true Church of God? 153
4. By what means is the Church of God built? 154
5. Wherein lies the power of the Church of God? 155
6. Why is church membership to be regarded as a privilege? 158
7. What blessings does proper church attendance bring? 63

COMMANDMENTS (cf. Law)

CONSCIENCE

1. What is conscience? 38
2. Why is conscience not an infallible guide of conduct? 38
3. What does conscience tell us about God? 26

CONVERSION (Regeneration)

1. What does conversion mean? 109–12
2. How do we become converted? 110
3. How does conversion affect our attitude toward God and His Law? 114, 139

COVETING

1. What does coveting mean? 84–85
2. What is the relation of coveting to all acts of sin? 85

CREATION

1. What is the meaning of the word "create"? 36
2. What is the relation between the Bible account of creation and the various evolutionary theories of creation? 35
3. What is the relation between human reason and the Bible account of creation? 36
4. Over what period of time was the world created? 36
5. What will happen to this creation at the end of time? 171

CROSS (of the Christian)

1. What is the meaning of bearing the cross after Jesus? 147–48
2. What is the purpose of the cross? 150
3. Why isn't the cross the same with all Christians? 148

DAMNATION

1. What is the state of damnation? 175–76
2. Who will suffer damnation? 175
3. What is the Bible's purpose in teaching the doctrine of damnation? 176

DEATH

1. What is meant by death? 168
2. What is the cause of death? 168
3. How does death affect man's continued existence? 169–70
4. What do the Scriptures teach regarding the death of Christ? 98
5. What does it mean that Christ redeemed us from death? 94, 97, 101

DESTINY

1. When is the eternal destiny of man decided? 170
2. What is the destiny of the Christian? 177–80
3. What is the destiny of the unbeliever? 175–76

DEVIL

1. Who is the devil? 40
2. How did the devil become an enemy of God? 40, 47
3. How was sin brought into the world by the devil? 48
4. What do the devil and his evil angels seek to do with the works of God? 40
5. What is the final fate of the devil and the evil angels? 174

DIVORCE

1. When according to the Scriptures is divorce permitted? 78
2. How are guilt and innocence determined in a divorce case? 78
3. What factors contribute to the high divorce rate in our day? 78–79
4. How does the law of the land often differ from the Law of God regarding divorce? 78

EXCOMMUNICATION

1. What is meant by excommunication? 157
2. Under what circumstances is excommunication to be applied? 157
3. What is the purpose of excommunication? 157

FAITH (of the Christian)

1. What is the meaning of Christian faith? 111
2. Who brings man to faith in God? 110
3. By what means is faith worked in man? 110
4. What is the relation of sincerity to Christian faith? 12

FATALISM

1. What is meant by fatalism? 43
2. Why is fatalism anti-Christian? 43

FORGIVENESS OF SINS (by God)

1. Why is the forgiveness of sins man's greatest need? 117
2. Why can God only forgive sins? 117

3. How much can man contribute toward his own forgiveness? 118

4. For whose sake and from what motive does God forgive sins? 118–19

5. How does Christ's redemptive work contribute toward man's forgiveness of sins? 119

6. What do we mean when we say that God forgives sins? 119

7. How is the forgiveness of sins proclaimed and promised to us? 119

8. For whom is forgiveness of sins available? 120

9. Who only receives forgiveness of sins from God? 120

10. How is our life to show and to prove that we have accepted the forgiveness of sins from God? 121

11. What place of importance does the forgiveness of sins hold in Christian preaching and teaching? 122

FORGIVENESS OF SINS (by Man)

1. To whom has God given the power to forgive sins, and what is this power called? 155

2. Why should we be forgiving toward our fellow men? 74, 129

3. What does it mean to be forgiving toward our fellow men? 74, 129

4. To whom is the forgiveness of sins to be declared? 155

5. To whom is the forgiveness of sins to be denied? 155

GAMBLING

1. Why is it sinful to gamble? 80

GOD

1. What is natural man's conception of God? 11, 23–24

2. What does nature reveal to us about God? 25

3. What does conscience tell us about God? 26

4. What, according to the Scriptures, are the attributes, or characteristics, of God? 27

5. What do the Scriptures teach about the oneness of God? 27

6. What do the Scriptures teach about the indivisible essence of God? 27

7. How is God unchangeable? 27

8. How is God infinite, or omnipresent? 27

9. How is God eternal? 27

10. What does it mean that God is a living, intelligent Being? 27

11. How is God omniscient? 27

12. How wise is God? 27

13. What does it mean that God has a will? 27

14. How is God holy? 27

15. How is God just and righteous? 27

16. How is God truthful? 27

17. What does it mean that God is almighty? 27

18. What does it mean that God is good? 27

19. What is meant by the triune God, or the Holy Trinity? 31

20. What do the Scriptures say about the Father being God? 31

21. What do the Scriptures say about Jesus Christ being God? 31, 92, 94

22. What do the Scriptures say about the Holy Spirit being God? 31

23. Why can't we understand the essence of God? 25, 32

24. What is God's relation to the world? 41–42, 90–91

GOOD WORKS (Sanctification of Life)

1. What is a good work in God's sight? 140–41

2. Why are non-Christians unable to do good works? 49, 141

3. In what sense are good works necessary and in what sense are they not necessary? 143

4. How does God reward us for doing good works? 144

GOSPEL

1. What is the Gospel? 14, 16, 91
2. How does the Gospel make Christianity different from all other religions? 15, 90
3. How does God use the Gospel to convert us? 91, 110, 154–56
4. How do we know that the Gospel invitation is always sincere and powerful? 91, 113
5. Why is the Gospel called a Means of Grace? 110, 113

GOVERNMENT OF GOD

1. What is meant by the government of God? 42
2. How does God use His creatures to govern the world? 41
3. How are the laws of nature used in God's government of the world? 42
4. What attributes of God are active in the government of God? 42
5. How does the Bible explain man's evil deeds in the face of God's government of the world? 42

HEAVEN

1. What do we mean by heaven? 177
2. Where is heaven? 179
3. Who will go to heaven? 177

HELL

1. What do we mean by hell? 175
2. Where is hell? 176
3. Who will go to hell? 175
4. What blessings are forever denied those in hell? 100, 175
5. When did Christ suffer the torment of hell for us? 98
6. What do the Scriptures teach regarding Christ's descent into hell? 100

HEREAFTER

1. What do we know about eternal life? 167

2. What does eternal life presuppose regarding the continued existence of this world? 171

3. What will be the condition of the Christians in the life to come? 173, 177

4. What will be the condition of the unbelievers in the life to come? 173, 175

5. How will the identity of man be affected in eternal life? 172

6. How will external conditions for the Christian in the life to come differ from conditions in the present world? 177

IDOLATRY

1. What is meant by idolatry? 23–25, 56–57

2. What is gross idolatry? 57

3. What is fine idolatry? 57

4. What forms of idolatry does natural man's conception of God take? 11

5. How does imagination affect idolatry? 25

INSPIRATION OF THE BIBLE

1. What claim for inspiration does the Bible make? 17

2. What is meant by inspiration? 17

3. What outside evidence is there for the inspiration of the Bible? 17

4. How did the inspired books of the Bible become recognized? 18

JUDGMENT (Final Judgment, Last Day)

1. What does the Bible teach about the fact, time, and place of the final judgment? 173

2. Who will be the Judge on Judgment Day? 103, 174

3. Who will be judged on Judgment Day? 174

4. On what basis will the judgment take place? 174

LABOR (Capital and Labor)

1. What is the duty of employer to employee? 70
2. What is the duty of employee to employer? 70
3. How can the employer-employee relationship be helped? 81
4. How does wholesome work keep us from temptation to evil? 80

LAW (The Ten Commandments)

1. Whose authority stands behind the moral law? 19, 53, 140
2. To what extent is the Law to be fulfilled? 53, 142
3. What is the threat to the transgressor of the Law? 54
4. What is the promise to the keeper of the Law? 54, 144
5. What is the purpose of the Law? 55, 87, 139
6. How does the Law show a perfect way to heaven? 89
7. Why is the way of salvation by the Law impossible to man? 89
8. How and for whom was Christ placed under the Law? 90
9. To what extent did Christ keep the Law for us? 89, 119
10. Why should Christians seek to keep the Law? 139, 143
11. To what extent can Christians keep the Law? 142
12. What is the First Table of the Law? 56
13. What is the Second Table of the Law? 66
14. Which is the First Commandment and its meaning? 56
15. Which is the Second Commandment and its meaning? 59
16. Which is the Third Commandment and its meaning? 62
17. Which is the Fourth Commandment and its meaning? 66
18. Which is the Fifth Commandment and its meaning? 71
19. Which is the Sixth Commandment and its meaning? 74
20. Which is the Seventh Commandment and its meaning? 80
21. Which is the Eighth Commandment and its meaning? 82
22. Which are the Ninth and Tenth Commandments and their meanings? 84

MAN

1. What do the Scriptures say about the creation of man? 37
2. What was the primeval state of man? 39
3. What caused man's fall into sin? 48
4. What is the religion of natural man since the fall into sin? 9–10, 89
5. How was the salvation of man accomplished? 89–92
6. When is the eternal destiny of man decided? 170
7. How does man become converted to God? 110
8. Why do not all men heed the invitation of the Gospel? 113
9. What is man's final destiny? 175–80

MARRIAGE

1. What is marriage? 74–76
2. What is the threefold purpose of marriage? 76
3. How important is the engagement, or betrothal? 75
4. What should be the relation of married people to each other? 77

MINISTRY (Public Ministry, Pastor)

1. What is the office of the public ministry? 68, 156
2. What should be our attitude toward our pastors? 64, 68, 156

NEIGHBOR

1. Who is our neighbor? 66
2. What are our responsibilities toward our neighbor? 66

OFFICE OF THE KEYS

1. What is the meaning of the Office of the Keys? 155
2. How is the Office of the Keys exercised? 155–56

PARENTS

1. What do parents owe to their children? 67
2. What do children owe to their parents? 67

PASTOR (cf. Ministry)

POSSESSIONS

1. Which are four honorable ways in which possessions may be secured? 80
2. What is the relation between poverty or wealth and morality? 136–37
3. How can material possessions be used properly? 81, 136–37

PRAYER

1. How is a life of prayer identified with Christianity? 61, 123
2. How are prayer and religion associated? 123
3. What may be the form of prayer? 123
4. What should be the content of prayer? 124
5. To whom alone should prayer be offered? 124
6. What is the basis of acceptable prayer before God? 124
7. What are the motives for prayer? 124
8. How will all proper prayers be answered? 126
9. For whom should prayers be offered? 126
10. How important are places of prayer? 127
11. How important is posture during prayer? 128
12. What is to be said about certain times for prayer? 128
13. What are the value and power of prayer? 128
14. What is the Lord's Prayer and its meaning? 129
15. How is prayer helpful in overcoming temptation to evil? 79

PURGATORY

1. What do Scriptures say about a purgatory? 170

RELIGION

1. What is religion? 9
2. Are Christianity and religion the same? 9

RESURRECTION

SABBATH

SACRAMENT

SACRAMENT OF HOLY BAPTISM (cf. Baptism)

SACRAMENT OF THE ALTAR

6. Why should we celebrate this Sacrament in remembrance of Christ? 164

7. Why should we commune frequently? 165

8. Which blessings are conveyed in this Sacrament? 165

9. Who is worthy and who is unworthy to partake of this Sacrament? 165–66

10. Why is a self-examination necessary before communing? 165

SALVATION

1. Why can't we be saved by the Law? 89

2. How did Christ secure salvation for us by means of the Law? 90

3. What prompted God to save us? 90

4. What do we mean when we say that salvation is an accomplished fact? 90

5. For whom is salvation available? 91

6. Is God concerned about the salvation of all mankind? 92, 120

7. Is the grace of God always powerful to save? 91

8. How should we show our gratitude to God for the salvation He has wrought for us? 44, 61, 107, 121, 124, 140, 144

9. On what is our hope of eternal salvation based? 121, 177

10. How may the state of bliss in eternal salvation be described? 177

11. What does God want us to do with the doctrine of salvation? 180

SEX

1. Why does the sex impulse lend itself so easily to abuse? 74–75

2. What is the meaning of adultery and fornication? 77

3. How may one overcome impure sexual thoughts and desires? 78

4. Who is to educate children in sex knowledge? 75

SIN

1. What is the meaning of sin? 47

2. What is the origin of sin? 47

3. Who brought sin into the world? 47–48

4. What are the consequences of sin? 48

5. Why is the corrupt condition of all mankind called the old Adam? 48

6. What are sins of commission? 49

7. What are sins of omission? 49, 73

8. What has been sin's effect on the natural knowledge of the Law? 50

9. How has sin been atoned for before the just and holy God? 89–92

10. How is God's forgiveness of our sin made known to us? 90, 119, 155

SOUL

1. What is a soul? 37, 169

2. Where are the souls of the dead? 169

3. What about a transmigration of souls and the possibility of the soul's return to this earth after a person dies? 170

4. When will the souls of the dead be reunited with their bodies? 172–73

5. What will be the state of restoration of the souls of Christians in the life hereafter? 178

STATE (Civil Government)

1. What is the purpose of civil government? 68

2. What is the duty of the state to the citizenry? 68

3. What is the duty of the citizens to the state? 68

STEWARDSHIP

1. What is the meaning of stewardship? 134

2. How does stewardship properly describe the state of the Christian before God? 134

3. What is the stewardship obligation of our social contacts? 134

4. What is the stewardship of our time? 135

5. How are good stewards to acquire material possessions? 136

6. How are good stewards to use their material possessions? 137

7. Which things deserve first place in our stewardship consideration? 136–38

8. What is the reward of faithful stewardship? 138